COOKERY

to save fuel and food value

Issued in the National Food Campaign Exhibition
1941

Rations
A Very Peculiar History™

With NO added butter

'Do not rest on your spades, except for those brief periods which are every gardener's privilege.'

Lord Woolton, Minister for Food.

For my grandchildren –
that they never go hungry

DA

Editor: Jamie Pitman
Additional artwork: David Antram, Carolyn Franklin

Published in Great Britain in MMX by
Book House, an imprint of
The Salariya Book Company Ltd
25 Marlborough Place, Brighton BN1 1UB

ISBN: 978-1-907184-25-3

7 9 8

A CIP catalogue record for this book is available
from the British Library.
Printed and bound in China.
Printed on paper from sustainable sources.
Reprinted in MMXVII

Visit
www.salariya.com
for our online catalogue and
free fun stuff.

WARNING: The Salariya Book Company accepts
no responsibility for the historical recipes in this
book. They are included only for their historical
interest and may not be suitable for modern use.

Rations
A Very Peculiar History™

With NO added butter

Written by
David Arscott

Illustrated by
Mark Bergin

Created and designed by
David Salariya

BOOK HOUSE
a SALARIYA imprint

'Dig for victory'
Ministry of Agriculture slogan
to promote the growing of food

'Doctor Carrot –
the children's best friend'
Government wartime slogan

'The ration book diet was difficult to
follow and was boring and monotonous,
but events have proved that it was
actually good for you.'
Cookery writer Marguerite Patten

'Make do and mend'
Government campaign to promote the
recycling of clothing and other materials

'When you feel tired of your old
clothes, remember that by making them
do you are contributing some part of an
aeroplane, a gun or a tank.'
The President of the Board of Trade

Contents

Your own vegetables all the year round...

if you

DIG FOR VICTORY NOW

YES, WE HAVE NO BANANAS!

For Britons, the nightly bombing raids were the very worst thing about the second world war, and stumbling about in the pitch darkness because of the blackout was a pretty grim experience, too – but can you imagine the endless dreariness of standing in queues every day in the hope of buying something that had probably run out long before you reached the shop door?

There were shortages of food, of clothes, of coal to keep warm (nearly everyone had a coal fire in those days) and even of comfortable chairs to sit on if your old one wore out.

The government introduced rationing at the beginning of 1940 in order to make things as fair as possible. Without it, rich people could have bought as much as they liked, and that would have left very little for everyone else.

There were, as we shall see, crafty ways of getting round the regulations, but by and large everyone suffered together.

And if they complained, there was a common, exasperated response: 'Don't you know there's a war on?'

Those queues

It's often said that the British habit of patiently and politely standing in line was learnt in wartime.

What's certainly true (it comes up in so many memoirs) is that people would often join a queue without any idea of what they might find at the end of it. Mothers would thrust money into their children's hands with strict instructions to bring home whatever they could afford.

Doing it by the book

Everyone had a ration book during the war – beige for adults, blue for school children and pink for babies and toddlers. You had to register with a local grocer and a local butcher, and they were the only shops from which you could buy rationed food.

The coupons in the book weren't a substitute for money. They simply allowed you to buy your fair share – assuming that you could afford it in the first place.

The amount everyone was allowed depended on how scarce or plentiful it was at the time, which meant that the quota might vary from one month to the next.

Meat was rationed by cost rather than weight, so that you could choose between a small cut of something expensive or a joint of something cheap.

A points system covered other items, such as canned food and clothing. Everyone had the same number of points, and (as with meat) you could splurge them on something special or eke them out to buy several smaller things – if you could find them!

And if they didn't need it? That wasn't a problem, because they could promptly sell it to someone who did – probably at a small profit.

A sense of humour helped people get by. Before the war there was a popular comic song called 'Yes, we have no bananas', and during the war shopkeepers would display the title in their windows, as bananas were a great rarity for years.

One shop, still operating despite a gaping hole in the wall after a bombing raid, sported a tongue-in-cheek notice which read 'Open for business'.

A royal dribble

King George VI and Queen Elizabeth set the nation a good example by living frugally at Buckingham Palace when they could have left London and lived safely on one of their country estates.

They even had a 5 inch (12.7 cm) line painted near the bottom of their bath to show how much water they should use.

One is accustomed to more than a drip...

Five inches of water could go a surprisingly long way.

No, there wasn't a shortage of water, but the government had suggested that 5 inches of water was how much a whole family should use in a week – between them! – in order to save the electricity used to heat it.

We don't know whether the king and queen followed this advice and shared their puddle, but when America's First Lady, Eleanor Roosevelt, visited the palace in the autumn of 1941 (shortly before the United States entered the war) she was shocked by the spartan conditions in which they were living.

The bath water was shallow, there was no heating and she found only one electric bulb in each room.

Yes, there was indeed a war on – but how had things become so very desperate?

WHY WE RAN SHORT

All countries import goods they can't make or grow themselves, but at the time war broke out Britain relied on other countries to a worrying degree. More than 50 million tons of food were being shipped in every year – and that amounted to a staggering 60 per cent of everything we ate.

Being an island meant that we couldn't easily be overrun by an invading army as so many European countries were from 1939 onwards, but it also left us dangerously isolated unless we could control the seas around us.

Germany's U-boats were responsible for many sunken trade ships.

Those waters were now patrolled by fast German E-boats carrying guns and torpedoes, while beneath the waves enemy U-boat submarines hunted our merchant vessels in deadly 'wolf packs' which would come to the surface at night to fire their torpedoes.

Many British cargo boats were needed to transport troops and to carry munitions and other material vital to the war effort. Others did continue to bring food to our shores, but in the early months of the war they were being destroyed at a frightening rate.

During the so-called Battle of the Atlantic, ships bringing food, fuel, equipment and raw materials from North America were being lost at the rate of sixty a month: the final toll was all of 2,500.

Some 30,000 Allied seamen perished while taking part in this epic struggle which was crucial to Britain's very survival.

No wonder Winston Churchill later wrote that 'the only thing that ever really frightened me during the war was the U-boat peril'.

Counting the pennies

If you began doing sums with money after the pound was divided into a hundred pennies in 1971 ('decimilisation') you may find some of the figures in this book rather confusing.

This is the system people had to cope with during the war years:

- The pound was divided into 20 shillings.
- The shilling – commonly called a 'bob' – was divided into 12 pennies, or pence, so that there were 240 pennies in a pound.
- The penny was divided into two half-pennies (or ha'pennies, pronounced *hay*-pennies) and four farthings (meaning 'fourths').

Your pockets soon wore out because there were so many different coins. The pound was available only as a note (there was a ten-shilling note, too), but the penny was large and heavy, and on top of the shilling, ha'penny and farthing there was a half-crown (two-and-a-half shillings), the florin (two shillings), the little silver sixpence – known as a 'tanner' – and the hexagonal three-penny (pronounced *thru*-penny) bit.

Phew!

Oh, and you also have to come to terms with the way the figures were written down, because they can look rather puzzling.

- The pound, as now, was a kind of 'L' (£) after the Latin 'librum'.

- The shilling could appear as an 's' (1s.), but you'll often find it shown as 1/-. If you come across, for example, 3/9, that means three shillings and nine pence – or 45 pence. (Wake up at the back, there!)

- The penny was written as a 'd', after the Latin 'denarius', so that two pence (known as 'tuppence') appears as 2d.

Here's a translation of the old money into today's currency:

Ten shillings = 50p
Five shillings = 25p
One shilling = 5p
Sixpence = 2.5p
A penny = not worth bothering about!

Beware of making simple comparisons, though. A pound would buy you a lot more in those days, but most people didn't have nearly as many of them in those threadbare pockets of theirs – a man's average weekly wage was less than £4.

You could buy a mountain of sweets with a pound note – but you'd never be given one!

Little by little the Allies learned to counter the U-boat threat. For one thing, ships now sailed together in convoys, escorted by small warships (Corvettes) and supported by long-range RAF Liberator marine patrol aircraft.

The code-breakers

And then, in May 1941, the Royal Navy captured one of the German submarines and seized its 'Enigma' machine. This was a device for scrambling messages into a code that was

Under the counter

Shopkeepers would often keep unrationed goods off the shelves, reserving them for their regular customers.

This wasn't illegal as long as they charged the price that had been fixed by the government to ensure that nobody made unreasonable profits at a time of severe shortages.

Hopeful customers would ask if there was anything 'under the counter'. Often there was nothing there at all – but it was certainly worthwhile making friends with your butcher and grocer just in case there was.

supposed to outwit the enemy, but a team of brilliant men and women at Bletchley Park in Buckinghamshire had worked out how to *un*scramble them.

The Allies could now tune in to German radio signals and work out the routes ships should take to avoid areas where the U-boats clustered in large numbers.

By May 1943 Admiral Dönitz, the German commander, had lost two-thirds of his submariners (some 28,000 men) and no fewer than 781 U-boats. He conceded defeat: the Battle of the Atlantic was over.

The good news was that more goods and equipment could now flow into Britain, whose heavily bombed population was quite literally feeling the pinch.

The bad news? There were still years of scrimping and saving ahead.

Never mind those bananas – there were shortages of practically all the foodstuffs people had once taken for granted.

National Registration Day

On Friday, September 29th 1939, every householder in Britain had to fill in a form with details of all the people who lived on the premises. It was a form of census.

Everyone was then issued with an identity card (a vital document in wartime) and a ration book – even more vital if you wanted to keep the family fed.

Rationing didn't actually begin until January 1940. Some felt the delay was caused by the *Daily Express* newspaper, which led a vigorous 'Stop rationing!' campaign, describing the system as 'government control gone mad'.

Most people approved of the idea, though, because they could see that it was fair.

CHAPTER TWO

WHALE MEAT AGAIN

Trust the British to make a joke of it: one of the most popular hits of the war years was Vera Lynn's 'We'll Meet Again', and in no time at all the ration-weary public had changed the words to reflect their sorry plight.

Yes, for them it was 'whale meat again', although you get the impression that nobody happily tucked into it more than once.

But as your favourite food disappeared from the shelves, you had to turn to the available substitutes or go hungry.

Imperial measurements

You'll find second world war recipes scattered throughout this book, so you need to know about 'imperial' measurements such as pounds and ounces. Back in the war years kilos and grammes were 'foreign' weights, and some older people today still find it hard to come to terms with the metric system – however simple it may seem to you.

Here's a rough-and-ready check-list:

> 1oz (ounce) = 25gm
> 1lb (pound or 16 ounces) = 450gm
> 1 fluid ounce = 25ml
> 1 pint = 450ml

And while we're at it, here are a few length conversions, too:

> 1 inch = 2.5cm
> 1ft (foot or 12 inches) = 0.3 metres
> 1 yard (three feet) = 0.9m
> 1 mile (1760 yards) = 1.6km

Not surprisingly, mothers sometimes wouldn't tell their children what they were eating until the meal was over.

Here are a few of the novelties that the British found on their plates:

- **Whale meat.** 'Best left swimming in the sea,' was a common reaction. It was a tough meat and, naturally, it had a fishy flavour.

- **Snoek.** Pronounced 'snook' to rhyme with 'book', this was canned fish (barracouta) imported from South Africa. Everyone seems to have hated it.

- **Horse meat.** This had previously been fed only to dogs, so butchers had to put 'fit for human consumption' notices on their counters.

- **Offal.** Animals' innards such as liver, kidneys and tripe. They can be part of a very tasty hotpot, but the very idea makes some people squirm.

- **Sheep's head.** No, you didn't eat the head itself, but a flavoursome dinner could be made by putting one in a pot with vegetables, so that you had – as one wartime child later remembered it – 'the teeth staring out from the stew mixed with all potatoes and carrots and dumplings'. Lovely!

- **Spam.** Largely made of pork, this arrived from the USA in tins. Many people found it lip-smacking – and you can still buy it today.

- **Dried egg powder.** Fine in a cake, but horrible in an omelette.

- **Pom.** Powdered spuds, mixed with water to make mashed potato.

- **Saccharine tablets.** An intensely sweet substitute for sugar.

- **Dried milk powder.**

Dripping (the fat from roast beef) was used as a substitute for butter: spread on toast, it was regarded by many as a delicious treat.

Chewing on wood

Sweets were very hard to come by. They went 'on the ration' in July 1942 and didn't come off it for more than ten years. A typical allowance – it varied – was a meagre 12oz (350gm) every four weeks, so children had to be thankful for what they could get.

One advantage of so-called 'Spanish wood' was that it lasted you a long time.

It was a stick of dried liquorice root, and the experience of eating it was rather like sinking your teeth into a slightly flavoured pencil.

Some children turned in desperation to Horlicks tablets, which weren't on the ration – and certainly weren't sweet in the slightest – and cough drops. *Ugh!*

Others would shake together cocoa and any sugar they could scrounge and call it 'chocolate mixture'.

Meanwhile, in Holland...

Britain wasn't the only country to suffer food shortages during the war.

Throughout what was known as 'the hunger winter' Dutch people were reduced to eating the tulip bulbs for which their country is famous.

These were roasted on stoves and turned out to be tasty enough. The trouble was that they gave people a nasty dose of indigestion.

All right for some

However fair the government tried to be, the fact is people in the countryside generally had a better way of life. Not only were they not being bombed, but they had a greater choice of food.

Pheasant and other game weren't rationed, which meant that a wealthy landowner could keep his larder well stocked. The salmon in his streams were off-ration, too, along with all the other bounty of his estate – eggs, milk, butter, bacon and so on.

Ordinary people in rural areas were often better off, even if they didn't farm the land themselves. They had more room to keep livestock and to grow extra vegetables – and if they weren't averse to a bit of poaching, they might add a rabbit or a pheasant to the evening stew as well.

Soon greengrocers from the towns who had sufficient petrol coupons (*see page 105*) were driving their lorries out into the country to buy vegetables direct from the growers there.

Lord Portly was furious
that there were no
quail's eggs for supper.

Eating out

Another way of bypassing the rationing problem was to eat away from home, whether at school, in an industrial canteen or (if you could afford it) at a posh restaurant.

You can imagine, though, that people who didn't have much to eat and whose houses were being blown up around their ears weren't amused to see 'toffs' enjoying the high

What wasn't rationed

Among the foodstuffs never rationed during the war were:

- **Bread.** There was only the National Loaf, made of wholemeal flour: most people preferred the old, less healthy white variety.

- **Vegetables.** Often in short supply.

- **Fruit.** Even more scarce.

- **Fish and chips.**

- **Beer**

life while everyone else was suffering, and there was an outcry against it.

The government quickly acted to head off this resentment. They prevented restaurants from charging more than 5s a meal (still a large amount in those days) and from serving both meat and fish dishes in one meal.

But not all restaurants were what would have been called 'swanky'. Local authorities ran so-called British Restaurants, often in schools and church halls, with a three-course meal costing only 9d.

Open to everyone, they attracted queues of people for their basic British fare of bangers and mash and comforting, stodgy puddings.

This was also the heyday of the nationwide Lyons' tea shops and corner houses, with their uniformed waitresses known as Nippies.

These were a little more expensive (1/6 for a three-course meal and a coffee), but they became popular meeting places for a broad cross-section of the public.

Woolton pie

Ingredients:

- 1lb each of diced potatoes, cauliflower, swedes and carrots
- three or four spring onions
- one teaspoonful of vegetable extract
- 1oz of oatmeal or rolled oats

Method:

- Dice and cook the potatoes, cauliflower, swedes and carrots in boiling salted water.
- Strain, but keep three-quarters of a pint of the vegetable water.
- Arrange the vegetables in a large pie dish or casserole. Add the vegetable extract and the rolled oats or oatmeal to the vegetable liquid.
- Cook until thickened and pour over the vegetables.
- Cover with potato pastry: take 4oz self-raising flour with a pinch of salt; rub in 1 to 2oz of fat; add 4oz of smooth mashed potato; use a little water to bind; and roll out as for ordinary short-crust pastry.

Lord Woolton to the rescue

The first foodstuffs to be rationed, on January 8th, 1940, were bacon, butter and sugar, and the list was steadily expanded over the following months and years.

By the end of the war it included all meat, tea, margarine, jam, cheese, eggs, rice, dried fruit, tinned tomatoes, peas, sweets, chocolate and biscuits.

Sausages weren't rationed, but you didn't always know what the butcher had put in them. (Yes, it could be whale meat!)

Lord Woolton, the Minister for Food, realised that the nation's health could suffer drastically if people failed to feed themselves properly, so he began a vigorous campaign aimed at the nation's cooks.

He gathered around him a team of nutritonists and home economists – one of the most famous being Marguerite Patten, whose version of the meatless 'ration-book recipe' in his honour appears on the opposite page.

The ministry produced recipe books whose offerings sounded less than appetising:

- vinegar cake
- fish-and-cabbage-spread sandwiches
- eggless fruit cake
- pilchard tart
- crumb fudge

They spread their message on a popular BBC 'wireless' programme called The Kitchen Front – the idea being that the nation's cooks were playing every bit as vital a role in the war effort as the soldiers firing bullets on the other front (the so-called Front Line).

Potato Pete and Doctor Carrot

Potatoes and carrots were plentiful, and they were each given a cartoon character to promote them.

Potato Pete, a cheery chappy in knee-length boots with a tiny hat perched on his head, had his own recipe book which included such delightful offerings as potato bread, potatoes on toast, champ (mashed potatoes with cabbage), potato drop scones and potato sandwich spread.

How much each?

Although the amount varied, here's a typical ration for one adult per week:

Butter: 50g (2oz)
Bacon and ham: 100g (4oz)
Margarine: 100g (4oz)
Sugar: 225g (8oz)
Meat: To the value of 1s 2d.
Milk: 3 pints.
Cheese: 2oz (50g)
Eggs: 1 fresh egg a week.
Tea: 50g (2oz)
Jam: 450g (1lb) every two months.
Dried eggs 1 packet every four weeks.
Sweets: 350g (12oz) every four weeks.

In addition, everyone was allowed 16 points each month to use as they wished.

There were also special allowances for pregnant women and breast-feeding mothers (extra milk and vitamins); children under 5 (seven pints of free or subsidised milk); and, after 1942, all children (orange juice and cod-liver oil).

'Doctors advise each of us to eat at least 12oz, and if possible 1lb of potatoes each day,' the introduction runs. 'Potatoes help save both fat and flour in pastries, puddings and cakes.'

You were supposed not only to cook potatoes with the skins on (of course), but to eat the leafy tops of turnips and carrots as well.

Unfortunately Pete and his ministry friends were responsible for some pretty dire versions of familiar nursery rhymes, such as:

> *Jack Spratt could eat no fat*
> *His wife could eat no lean;*
> *So they both ate potatoes*
> *And scraped their platters clean.*

'Simple but better fare is the aim of the new cookery,' wrote the compiler of a *Daily Telegraph* cookery book. One of her recipes is reproduced on the facing page.

'New times necessitate new cookery. The old cookery books have become out of date for application to the tables, larders and store-cupboards of a changing world.'

Baked Potato Pudding

Ingredients:

- ½lb smoothly mashed potato
- 1½oz caster sugar
- 2oz currants
- 2oz margarine
- lemon substitute equivalent to 1 lemon
- 1 egg
- milk

Method:

- Cream fat and sugar.
- Mix in mashed potato with well-beaten egg and sufficient milk to make a soft mixture.
- Add lemon substitute (such as apple peel) and currants.
- Mix thoroughly and bake in greased pie dish in moderate oven for 45 minutes.

Everyone knew what that meant: create weird concoctions from whatever ingredients you could conceivably mix together to make something slightly recognisable from the period before the war!

Doctor Carrot was every bit as active as Pete, but he went one better by having some family members invented by the famous American animator Walt Disney. These were Pop Carrot, Clara Carrot and Carroty George.

The official line was that 'carrots keep you healthy and help you see in the blackout'.

True? Well, they contain vitamin A, and that's good for your eyes and skin, but munch too many of them and you'll end up looking the colour of a carrot yourself.

Some people later claimed the 'seeing in the dark' myth was a government ploy to hide the secret of British radar from the Germans. Our flying ace 'Cat's Eyes Cunningham' targeted enemy aircraft with the aid of radar beams, but it was useful to put his deadly aim down to a diet of carrots.

Folk often wondered, 'If he's so good for your eyesight, why does he wear glasses?'

Ten things to make with carrots

- **Carrolade.** A drink of carrot juice and grated swede squeezed through a piece of muslin. (Try this one at home only if you're very brave.)

- **Carrot cakes.** Some mistake, surely. These are delicious!

- **Carrot croquettes.**

- **Carrot fudge.**

- **Carrot jam.**

- **Carrot pudding.**

- **Curried carrots.**

- **Mock apricot tarts.**

- **Potato and carrot pancakes.**

- **Toffee carrots.**

Once regarded as suitable only for animal feed, the humble carrot had become the most common ingredient in British cookery and was being grown in huge quantities.

Indeed, so successful was the government's drive for extra production that by the beginning of 1942 there was a glut of them – about 100,000 tons more than were needed. What on earth could be done with so many surplus carrots?

Meanwhile, in America...

Chewing gum became an official 'war material', thanks to the advertising skill of a leading maker of the stuff, Philip K. Wrigley.

He persuaded the US authorities that it relieved soldiers' tension, slaked their thirst and even cleaned their teeth – and he was asked by the army to supply a stick of gum for every pack of their combat rations.

American soldiers (GIs) in Britain became used to hopeful children calling out to them, 'Got any gum, chum?'

Yes, you've guessed it: they were used as animal feed as before! They were an excellent food for dairy cows and horses, and they helped fatten up pigs and bullocks.

There was a problem, though. Crooked dealers might sell them to shops and restaurants, making an illegal profit, so the government sprayed the surplus carrots with a (harmless) violet dye.

Poster power

'As many a wise mother knows,' declared an official cookery leaflet, 'the child who eats raw carrot freely is most unlikely to have a craving for sweets.'

That was the kind of half-truth put about by the government during the war. (After all, you might like raw carrots *and* go mad for a bar of chocolate, mightn't you?)

It reinforced simple messages like this with a vast array of colourful posters, some of them designed by famous artists who had been drafted in to help the war effort.

Preventing waste was a theme of several of them:

- Waste not, want not.

- A clear plate means a clear conscience.

- Food is a munition of war – don't waste it.

- Better pot-luck with Churchill today than humble pie under Hitler tomorrow: Don't waste food!

As the first organisation in the world to provide advice on healthy eating, the Ministry of Food naturally had plenty of posters to promote that, too.

And here's the amazing thing: after all those years of deprivation and of making do with what little they could get, the British people were in general more healthy at the end of the war than their descendants (us) are today.

Luckily the moral of this isn't that we should eat whale meat and drink Carrolade (phew!) but that as a nation we ought to consume less meat and fat and more fruit and vegetables.

Potato Pete was right after all . . .

first catch your squirrel

The BBC's Home Service programme 'The Kitchen Front' encouraged listeners to send in ideas for economy dishes.

Pigs' brains and cows' udders were suggested as useful ingredients (let us know how you get on with them), while other recipes included:

- Crow pie
- Rosehip chutney
- Sheep's head broth
- Squirrel tail soup

Dig for Victory

The solution to the shortages problem was obvious – we should grow more ourselves. And that's what we did, very quickly and on an enormous scale.

Farmers were paid to cultivate much more of their land (they'd have it taken over, or 'requisitioned', if they didn't), and this often meant taking the plough to poor soil and hilly areas that hadn't been regarded as suitable before. Many of them worked through the night at it.

The government aimed to have an extra 1,700,000 acres (688,000 hectares, or the equivalent of about a million football pitches) ready for production by harvest time 1940. Incredibly, they reached their target in April, several months ahead of schedule.

The 'Plough Now' campaign was nationwide. Every county appointed a War Agricultural (War Ag) Committee tasked with finding as much spare land as it could to grow vegetables and cereals.

Gourmet chefs of the future would probably disagree.

But the job of feeding the nation wasn't to be left to the professionals – the farmers. There was a vital role for amateurs to play, too.

'We want not only the big man with the plough,' said the Minister for Agriculture, Rob Hudson, in October 1939, 'but the little man with the spade to get busy this autumn. Let *Dig for Victory* be the motto of everyone with a garden.'

So it was that lawns and flower beds all over the country were swiftly turned into miniature allotments, and that many men, women and children who had never previously handled a trowel or a hoe found themselves sowing seeds and harvesting crops.

Gardens made obvious plots, but many other areas were dug up at the same time:

• tennis courts and golf courses
• parks and recreation grounds
• railway embankments
• seaside promenades
• bombsites
• the Tower of London moat

Soon there were 1.5 million allotment holders throughout the country, producing 10 per cent of the nation's food. This army of novice labourers needed advice about tilling the soil, and experts were on hand to guide them.

Families would gather round their wireless set just before lunch every Sunday to hear C.H. Middleton give his growing, harvesting and storing tips. With an audience of some three million, he was broadcasting's first ever 'celebrity gardener'.

Poor Chad goes without

A little cartoon character called Chad popped up all over the place during the war as a kind of humorous protest about shortages.

He was depicted looking over a wall, and his message always began 'Wot, no . . .'

Wot, no pork chops?

As plain 'Mr Middleton' he wrote a *Digging for Victory* book ('the harder we dig for victory the sooner will the roses be with us'), while the government poured out a stream of pamphlets, booklets and posters.

Here are the titles of some exciting sounding ministry leaflets:

- Cropping Plan for a Ten-Rod Plot (250m²)
- How to Make a Compost Heap
- How to Sow Seeds
- Pests and Diseases in the Vegetable Garden
- Preserves from the Garden
- Seed Potatoes

And here's a jolly victory anthem that was played on the radio:

Dig! Dig! Dig! And your muscles will grow big
Keep on pushing the spade
Don't mind the worms
Just ignore their squirms
And when your back aches laugh with glee
And keep on diggin'!

Try it on your friends – and run!

Gardeners as well as cooks were regarded as being on the Kitchen Front, and they were given a rousing 'pep-talk' in a government brochure:

- Women must help. They make good gardeners and can do much of the work – getting the older children to help them.

- Onions have been as rare as diamonds. Potatoes, too, have at times been scarce. Make sure of getting them by growing them yourself.

- Every row of potatoes – every row of cabbage – helps your family and your country. Flowers add nothing to the nation's 'growing' power.

- To grow vegetables for winter and summer you must have a plan – or you will have a summer glut and bare ground all the winter.

- Thousands of people have discovered that a 10-rod (0.025 hectare) plot will keep a family of five in vegetables for eight months of the year.

- Food is just as important a weapon of war as guns.

To retain a lawn, let alone a flower bed, was regarded as pretty selfish behaviour, so most disappeared – meaning that children lost their accustomed play areas. As we've seen, the local park was probably churned up for vegetables, too.

People would strenuously break up their concrete yards in order to create new vegetable patches, and even the roof of an Anderson shelter could be given a topping of soil and planted with lettuces and cabbages.

follow that horse!

All the freshly dug earth in gardens, parks and playing fields which had never been cultivated before needed a lot of manure to enrich it.

Luckily there was a ready supply brought almost to your doorstep every day – and it was completely free!

In the war years most of the tradesmen's carts (butcher, baker, milkman) were drawn by horses, and youngsters would be sent out into the streets with shovels to scoop up what they left behind.

Sausage Pancakes

Ingredients:

- 1lb small sausages
- 4oz flour
- ½ pint milk
- ½oz custard powder
- salt and pepper

Method:

- Mix together the custard powder and the flour, then mix with some milk to make a smooth batter.
- Beat well for five minutes.
- Stir in the rest of the milk.
- Season with salt and pepper and leave to one side.
- Fry the sausages, remove from pan and keep hot.
- Pour off some of the fat and save, leaving enough in the pan to fry the first pancake.
- Brown the pancake lightly on both sides and roll up with the sausage inside. Keep warm.
- Add some of the saved fat to the frying pan and add more batter for further pancakes.

While the vast majority of these gardening beginners followed the rules and grew the obvious things, some were tempted to produce something more exotic.

As smoking was much more widespread in the war years, and cigarettes were in short supply, it's perhaps not surprising that a few men who were 'gasping for a fag' decided to grow their own tobacco and hang the leaves up to dry. (Apparently it was better than nothing.)

The BBC's radio doctor, Charles Hill – the author of *Wise Eating in Wartime* – gave regular advice on healthy eating, and his tips weren't always welcomed by the younger members of his audience.

Thanks to him, many a child was subjected to daily helpings of shredded raw cabbage, while prunes were recommended in support of his customary signing-off line: 'Keep the bowels well open!'

Oh, and another radio programme, just before school, put the nation's children through a brisk regime of healthy exercises, too.

Gardening was hard work, and you had to buy the seeds and tubers first, so it was very satisfying if you could go out foraging to increase your supplies.

This sometimes meant 'scrumping' apples and other fruit from neighbours' trees (and risking a clip round the ear for your trouble), but there was often legitimate 'food for free' around the corner if only you knew where to look for it and what to do with it – and there was government advice here, too.

Marrow liqueur

Marrows sprouted everywhere on wartime allotments, and they were often included in recipes, but if you think there's not much to be said for them as a vegetable you'll perhaps understand why some men put them to a different use altogether.

They would cut one end, scoop out the pulp, fill it with sugar, bore a hole in the bottom end and hang it up for several weeks, letting the liquid drip into a jar.

It made a kind of marrow brandy!

In the countryside, of course, there were plentiful supplies of nuts and berries in the hedgerows and mushrooms in the fields which the locals were used to harvesting. But, as the official 'Food Facts' leaflets explained, there was a wide range of edible vegetation even in and around the towns.

As part of the war effort families would set out in group forays to bring back not only plump blackberries but stinging nettles, dandelion leaves, sloes and crab apples.

There was also a national drive to pick rosehips (if you were lucky you'd be paid for the effort), and these eager bands of collectors picked enough to provide all the health-giving rosehip syrup, rich in vitamin C, that was needed during the war years.

Gathering rosehips from the bushes was a rather painful business because of all the thorns, but for pesky schoolboys the scratches on their legs (they all wore shorts in those days) were a small price to pay for the pleasure of tormenting girls with the fruit. You can probably guess how.

They would take a few rosehips home in their pockets, break them open in the classroom, drop the seeds down the back of an unsuspecting girl's dress – and wait for the howls. They do make a very effective itching powder!

Even the humble acorn was worth collecting, because farmers would pay so much a bag in order to feed their pigs.

It was one thing to grow and harvest food during the summer and autumn months, but the new army of gardeners and cooks needed instructions on how to preserve it for use during the long winter months.

The government, as ever, issued a flurry of leaflets with ideas for making things last longer. These included:

• Bottling fruit
• Pickling eggs and onions
• Salting beans
• Making jam

Edith didn't know
whether to wear
it or eat it.

The overriding message was that nothing should be wasted. If it was edible and you had too much of it – preserve it. If it would rot down to feed the soil – put it on the compost heap. If it was a cabbage stump or a potato peeling – put it in a bin for the pigs.

Millions of post-war children grew up with tiresome parents and grandparents who tut-tutted about every left-over morsel on their plates. Now you know why . . .

Meanwhile, in Russia...

The terrible seige of Leningrad by the German Army during the winter of 1941–1942 puts the rationing in Britain into stark perspective.

Whereas the British suffered inconvenient shortages of many foodstuffs, the Russian people experienced horrific starvation as they were trapped in their city during a long period of intense cold.

At the height of the seige 10,000 people died of starvation every day. Some ate their pet animals, while others desperately ripped off their wallpaper in order to suck the glue.

The Women's Land Army

With the huge expansion of land now used for agriculture, and with the disappearance to the Front of 50,000 men who had previously worked on the farms, the call went out for what were to become known as 'land girls'.

The recruiting campaign for the Women's Land Army (WLA) trumpeted 'a happy, healthy life', and at its peak in 1943 some 80,000 women were digging, sowing and driving tractors. It was to be a rather tougher life than some of them had imagined.

An article in *Picture Post* magazine, in January 1940, highlighted a training centre to which 180 recruits were sent, their ages ranging from 18 to 53 years old.

Only one was a farmer's daughter. The rest – thirty-eight different peace-time occupations between them – included librarians, shorthand typists, chauffeuses, dressmakers, actresses, hairdressers, governesses, an artist, a poetess and one who registered herself simply as a 'television girl'.

They were often given back-breaking work to do, including:

- Ditching
- Hedging
- Muck-spreading
- Ploughing
- Planting
- Digging up potatoes
- Harvesting fruit
- Haymaking
- Threshing

Another of their jobs was rat-catching, and they had to tie strings around their trouser legs so that the wretched rodents didn't run up inside them. (Don't think about it.)

Trousers? Well, obviously they had to be appropriately dressed, and their kit included fawn shirts, corduroy breeches, a pair of dungarees (often rolled up into shorts), a brown felt hat (rather like a cowboy hat) and a pair of black rubber gumboots.

Unfortunately there was a shortage of boots after the Japanese invaded Malaya and Burma in December 1941, because this cut off rubber supplies, and the WLA magazine *The Land Girl* gave advice on how to preserve them for as long as possible. If they were damaged they had to be sent off to the Dunlop Rubber Company for repair.

Some of the girls joined a special Women's Timber Corps, their job being to cut down trees and work in sawmills. Can you guess what they were jokingly called?

A Land Girl doing her bit

Lumberjills, of course, after their male counterparts, lumberjacks!

Here's an inspiring hymn to these doughty ladies, courtesy of two WLA volunteers, P. Adkins and J. Moncrieff:

Back to the Land, we just all lend a hand,
To the farms and the fields we must go.
There's a job to be done,
Though we can't fire a gun,
We can still do our bit with the hoe.

A princess at the helm

Some complained that the WLA was regarded as a 'cinderella' organisation – that it wasn't regarded seriously enough – but it did have a real princess at the head of it.

Our present Queen, then the teenage Princess Elizabeth, served as its patron throughout the war.

In a Christmas message in 1941 she told the land girls that their skill and devotion had 'released great battalions of men who now fight for the land they formerly tilled'.

As we've seen, they did much more than hoeing, yet for all their labours they were paid no more than 28s a week (pretty poor even then) for working 48 hours a week and more.

Many came from the bright lights of a town to live in a hostel or in a run-down farmworker's cottage with no running water, gas or electricity. They had to get up before dawn and work in all weathers. They were allowed only a half-day off a week (not necessarily on a Saturday) and had a startling entitlement of just three days' holiday with pay after working six months for the same employer.

A handbook written for the new volunteer suggested that 'as the other girls from the village do not use make-up, she will prefer not to use it herself, so as not to look conspicuous. She will find, too, that she will get such a healthy colour to her cheeks that roughing will not be necessary.'

Was it worth it for the women themselves? Well, many of them later looked back on their agricultural days with real fondness, adding that they'd never been fitter in their lives.

And for the country as a whole? At first some farmers doubted that their new workers would be any good at all – the 'fair sex' was generally felt to be physically weak and ineffectual in those days – but by the end of the war the farm worker's union was begging them to stay.

After all, they had helped transform British agriculture, which was now producing huge amounts more than before. Here are some figures for the acres given over to crops at the beginning and end of the war.

	1939	1945
Wheat	1,760,000	2,274,000
Barley	1,013,000	2,215,000
Oats	2,427,000	3,753,000
Potatoes	704,000	1,397,000
Vegetables	291,000	512,000

But there's a sad end to the story. When the war was over the land girls were, indeed, treated like cinderellas and were refused the 'thank you' payment given to women working in state-employed services. Their honorary director, Lady Denman, resigned in protest.

Animals in your garden

You may have an image in your mind of wartime gardens given over to nothing but row upon row of vegetables. If so, please try to rearrange this mental picture to squeeze in a rabbit hutch or two, a chicken run and perhaps even the odd shed for a fattening pig. And is that a goat ready for milking that we see tethered to the fence post?

Yes, the government was keen to turn people not only into gardeners but into smallholders, or part-time farmers, as well.

As usual there was plenty of advice for the complete beginner, which was just as well – it's one thing to sow a row of beans; quite another to deal with a stubborn sow.

Chickens

The average size of a flock of hens was six. The advice was to get the birds from a registered dealer, and the most popular breed was a cross between the Black Leghorn (which gave a lot of eggs) and a Rhode Island Red (which was known for its hardiness).

The authors of the government booklet *Keeping Poultry and Rabbits on Scrap* reassured householders that 'there is no known waste from human edible food which is harmful in moderation.'

'Do not be content with using your own scraps,' they added. 'Get others to save for you. There are plenty of people too busily occupied, or maybe some too lazy and unpatriotic, to exert themselves, and undertake any work of national importance.'

That was telling 'em!

Nothing was simple in wartime. To get the wire to make your run you first had to show an official your chicken feed ration book. This entitled you to a weekly amount of mash to supplement what you had boiled up from your kitchen waste, but in return you had to give up at least part of your egg ration.

This may sound harsh, but it was perfectly fair. The egg ration (when they were available) was about one egg per week per person, whereas a chicken might lay 180 eggs in a year. Six of them would bring you more than a thousand eggs or about twenty a week. (You stored them in an isinglass jelly.)

By the end of the war the Domestic Poultry Keepers' Council had well over a million members who between them owned no fewer than 12 million birds.

Once the hens were too old for laying they could be fattened up and eaten, but many people found this impossible: the children had given them all names and had come to regard them as pets. They would be sold to friends or neighbours who were less squeamish about it.

But even if you *were* happy to put Chirpy and Cheeky in the oven, the business of killing them wasn't easy for some. Have you ever wrung a chicken's neck? Stories abound of failed attempts to do it properly, and we won't go into them here.

Rabbits

It wasn't much easier to say goodbye to a familiar rabbit, but at least that's why they were bought in the first place. Soon the nation's garden were littered with their runs – and running with their litters.

Countryfolk had always enjoyed a rabbit, of course, and they were plentiful out in the fields, but people in the towns took some persuading. Still, if it was a choice between eating rabbit and going hungry, there wasn't much of an argument against them.

Run, Rabbit, Run

Here's a hit song from the Blitz, made famous by Bud Flanagan and Chesney Allen.

On the farm, ev'ry Friday,
On the farm it's rabbit pie day,
So ev'ry Friday that ever comes along
I get up early and sing this little song.

Run, rabbit, run, rabbit, run, run, run
Run, rabbit, run, rabbit, run, run, run.
Bang, bang, bang, bang! goes the farmer's gun
Run, rabbit, run, rabbit, run, run, run!

On the farm, no poor rabbit
Comes to harm, because I grab it,
They jump and frolic whenever I go by.
They know I help 'em to dodge the rabbit pie.

Run, rabbit, run, rabbit, run, run, run
Don't give the farmer his fun, fun, fun
He'll get by without his rabbit pie,
So run, rabbit, run, rabbit, run, run, run!

Rabbit Stew

Ingredients:

- 1 whole rabbit, cut into joints
- 1 tbsp vinegar
- 1oz flour
- salt & pepper
- 1–2oz dripping
- 2 bacon rashers, de-rinded and chopped (if available)
- 2 medium onions, sliced
- 3 medium carrots, sliced
- 1 pint (600ml) water or stock
- 1 cooking apple
- fresh herbs (as available)

Method:

- Put the rabbit to soak in cold water with the vinegar for 30 minutes.
- Remove and dry well.
- Mix the flour with the salt and pepper and coat the rabbit joints.
- Heat the dripping and add the bacon rinds.
- Add the rabbit joints and cook steadily for about 10 minutes or until golden brown in colour.
- Remove from the pan.
- Add the bacon, onions and carrots and cook for 5 minutes, then return the rabbit to the pan.
- Add the water or stock and the grated apple and stir as the liquid comes to the boil and thickens slightly.
- Add the herbs.
- Bring to the boil and simmer for 30 minutes.
- Quickly put dish into the hay box and leave for 4 to 5 hours.
- Serve with seasonal vegetables.

You qualified for a bran ration if you joined a local rabbit club (there were thousands of them all over the country), but you were then supposed to offer half of your brood to the local butcher in compensation – although he couldn't possibly know how your breeding programme was coming along.

Fortunately, however, your unfussy bunnies were very happy munching scraps from the kitchen and any humble weeds you collected for them by the wayside.

Wingless chicken

Wild rabbit has an unmistakably gamey flavour, but the domesticated variety tastes much milder. This enabled parents to pass it off as chicken, although if it was one of their own rabbits they would have to make up a convincing story about its disappearance from the hutch – perhaps someone had come into the garden and stolen it.

It was far less excusable for a restaurant to charge its customers for chicken and serve them rabbit, but that did sometimes happen. One lad later remembered making a useful income from selling rabbits to the local chef.

Rabbit wasn't 'on the ration', so you could breed as many as you wished for the pot without giving up any coupons. If you had too many (and we all know how fast they breed) you could make a useful income by selling them at the local market or to a butcher.

Pigs

Keeping a pig in the garden was a rather more serious proposition, so many people who fancied pork in their diet joined one of the thriving pig clubs, of which there were 7,000 throughout the country. Schools sometimes ran them.

Your membership involved an initial cash fee and then some of the responsibility for looking after them. Your reward was a share of the pork and bacon when the pigs were killed. (No, you didn't have to wield the knife, thank goodness, although you did have to give up some of your meat ration, and half the carcasses had to be sold to the government.)

There were swill bins on street corners, with notices such as 'Feed a pig and beat Hitler' on them, and once they were full the contents were delivered to the clubs. Pigs will eat just about anything, so people threw every kind of kitchen waste in them – and they gave off a strong stench in hot weather.

Pigs themselves can be fairly smelly, but that didn't stop some people getting a licence to rear them in their gardens. After all, the government posters urged people to 'Keep a pig – save waste and make food'.

Neighbours wouldn't usually object, because they would often provide their kitchen scraps for pig food and would probably be offered a few cuts of the animal when it came to be killed.

The pig-keeping rules were strict, and you had to tell the authorities how many piglets you had in a litter, but sometimes one would go missing before the inspector came to call – and if, suitably fattened, it eventually found its way to the local butcher you might just expect a joint of pork by way of a reward.

Everything but its squeak

For butchers the pig is the most versatile of creatures, and they used to say that you could eat 'everything but its squeak'. Here are a few of the less familiar bits of it that people would use in wartime.

- **blood** (to make black pudding)
- **brains**
- **cheeks** (bought with the teeth embedded)
- **ears** (stuffed or crisped in breadcrumbs)
- **head** (in a stew, or boiled and seasoned to make 'brawn' to spread on sandwiches)
- **heart**
- **hocks** (ankles; with the head to make brawn)
- **intestines** (known as chitterlings)
- **kidneys**
- **liver**
- **snout** (boiled for two hours)
- **stomach** ('hodge')
- **tail** (roasted until crispy)
- **trotters** (jellied)

The lungs and stomach would be boiled and fed to dogs and cats, while the bladder made a good football.

How's your appetite?!

Rashers on the ration – good news for Porky and Porkette.

One man rang his doctor and asked him to make an urgent house call, adding mysteriously that his problem wasn't a medical one.

When the doctor arrived he was told that there had been an 'accident'. The man had a licence to kill one pig but had unfortunately killed two – it was called slaughtering two pigs with one squeak – and he needed to get the second one off the premises before the inspector arrived.

The kindly doctor took the carcass away and sold cuts of it to the patients he visited later in the day, asking them to pay whatever they felt was reasonable.

When he handed the cash to the pig's owner that evening he was told he had made a much bigger profit than if the man had sold it himself on the black market.

'We should go into business together!' he laughed.

A private function

Keeping a pig illegally at a time of rationing is the subject of the comedy film *A Private Function*, scripted by Alan Bennett and starring Maggie Smith and Michael Palin.

It's set just after the war, in 1947. Meat rationing is still in force, and an unregistered pig named Betty is being fattened up to feed diners at a civic function to celebrate the wedding of Princess Elizabeth.

The Palin character decides to steal it – with, of course, disastrous results.

Meanwhile, in Germany...

The Germans were forced to introduce food rationing, too, and it grew more severe as the war progressed.

Meat was in short supply and, as in England, many people kept rabbits – with children being given the job of looking after them.

Luxuries such as chocolate, whipped cream and cream cakes disappeared from the shelves. Because coffee was scarce (they drank a lot of it) people made substitutes from roasted barley seeds and even from acorns.

Enough to eat

The drive to make Britain more self-sufficient in food was a great success. At the outbreak of war we'd been importing 60 per cent of our food: by 1942 that figure had been cut in half, and this was followed by bumper harvests in 1943 and 1944.

Although the nation's intake wasn't perfect (it was high in carbohydrates and low in vitamin D, causing outbreaks of rickets in some areas) its overall health had, as we've seen, actually improved – with people getting more essential vitamins.

The Ministry of Food's verdict was clear. People were eating a more balanced diet and were drinking less; they were generally healthier although they had lost weight.

Ah, but that raised another little problem. In prosperous times you popped out and bought yourself a new set of clothes if your weight came down.

Not now! Clothes, too, were on the ration...

How clothes rationing worked

As with food rationing, the coupons in your book had no value in themselves: they simply showed how much you were allowed to buy if you could afford it.

The government didn't want everyone using up all their coupons at once, so they gave them different colours and gradually introduced each in turn. You could save coupons in the previous colour range for later on, but you couldn't use those that hadn't yet been given the go-ahead.

At first everyone was given a book of 66 coupons, but as materials became even more scarce this was reduced to 48 in 1942 and 36 in 1943. These had to last you for a whole year. (*See page 80 for what that meant.*)

There were a few extra coupons for women about to get married so that they could buy a basic wedding outfit, and for pregnant women so that they could buy nappies for their babies.

Children were also given a few extra points to allow for the fact that they were growing – but many had to get used to wearing hand-me-downs until well after the war was over.

CHAPTER THREE

MARRIED IN A PARACHUTE

f the bride wore a shimmering silk dress for her wartime wedding, the chances are that it was made from the remains of a discarded parachute.

Not very romantic, you might think – but when most of her friends had to go to the altar in something non-white and all too obviously inexpensive the lucky girl would have regarded it with absolute delight.

Clothes rationing was introduced on June 1st, 1941, largely for the same reason as the restrictions covering food. Wool and cotton were imported, and supplies had dried up.

What your coupons bought

We've seen on page 78 how many clothes coupons you were allowed each year (the number dropped from 66 to 36 over the space of just a year, between 1942 and 1943). Here's a list of how many of them were used up by each item of clothing.

Could you have coped?

	Men	Women	Children
Boots/shoes	7	5	3
Handkerchief	1	1	1
Jacket	13	12	8
Jumper/ cardigan	5	5	3
Overcoat	7	7	4
Pyjamas/ nightdress	8	6	6
Raincoat	16	15	11
Shirt/blouse	5	4	3
Shorts	3	3	2
Skirt	–	8	6
Socks/ stockings	2	2	1
Trousers	8	8	6
Underpants/ knickers/vest	3	3	2

In addition to that, able-bodied workers were needed in the factories for making more important things than clothes.

Parachutes, for example!

With material so scarce, you can understand why when a parachute or a barrage balloon came down there was often a race between local people and the authorities to see who could get to the scene first. The balloons could be cut up to make mackintoshes, while parachutes were fashioned into women's underwear as well as wedding dresses.

Decent clothes at an affordable price were hard to get, so in the spring of 1942 the government introduced the idea of 'utility' clothing, made from a limited range of materials, to specified standards and at fixed prices up to a third cheaper than their high street equivalents.

This proved popular and, since the designs weren't fixed, some well-known fashion houses jumped on the bandwagon and made their own versions.

There were strict rules governing new clothing. Men's trousers were to have no turn-ups because that was a waste of material, although if you had a friendly tailor he might give you extra length in the legs and advise you how to turn the bottoms up.

The jacket must be single-breasted, and have no more than three buttons and three pockets (although it could sport false pockets just for show). There was also a maximum length for men's shirts.

Meanwhile, in France...

Leather was in such short supply that the French produced 24 million pairs of wooden-soled shoes every year.

Their clattering on the pavements became one of the most familiar sounds of the war – and the famous singer Maurice Chevalier popularised a song called *Symphonie des Semelles de Bois*, or 'Symphony of the Wooden Soles'.

Ten strange ways to get by

There were tips galore on coping with the shortages of clothes and fabric during the war:

1. Varnish the soles of children's shoes to make them last longer.

2. Cut the toes from shoes when children outgrow them and call them sandals.

3. Cut up old mackintoshes to make bibs.

4. Cut up surgical lint to make nappies.

5. Make squares out of old stockings to use as dishcloths.

6. Create jewellery from beer bottle tops, cup hooks and corks, or from milk bottle tops covered with raffia.

7. Turn an old felt hat into bedroom slippers.

8. Bleach a flour bag to make a tablecloth.

9. White-wash newspapers for schools to use in art lessons.

10. Cut newspapers into squares to use as lavatory paper.

Women's clothes weren't allowed to have any unnecessary pleats, tucks, folds or gathers, let alone such extravagances as embroidery or sequins. Skirts were narrow, and hemlines rose to just below the knee. Even underwear was limited to six shapes which had been designed specifically to save material.

It was possible to buy dresses that were 'off coupon', but a desperate young woman tempted to buy one was likely to discover, on trying it on at home, that it was made of dyed hessian – a horribly cheap and itchy material best used for making sacks to store potatoes.

And then there was the elastic problem. Not only was it of a pretty poor standard, but there wasn't much of it around. We hope this doesn't make you blush, but some young women had to share one length of it among several pairs of knickers. When one pair went into the wash, out came the elastic to be inserted into the next one. Well, really!

All this made it a bit of a challenge for a bright young thing who wanted to make a good impression when 'out on the town'.

Siren suits

Perhaps because uniforms were common in wartime, people were quite happy to appear in public in 'siren suits', those baggy jumpsuits that would make you look rather like a 1940s Teletubby.

Winston Churchill often wore one, and even the two princesses Elizabeth and Margaret were seen in them.

The suits were practical in draughty conditions, and people would often throw them on before rushing to an air raid shelter in the Blitz.

Winston Churchill wears his siren suit with pride.

Stockings were scarce, and it was common for women to dye their legs with gravy browning and then draw a fake seam up the back with an eyebrow pencil. (The gunk had to be washed off before she went to bed unless she wanted to smell like a well-cooked stew.) An alternative to the gravy was a mixture of shoe polish and face cream, but that doesn't sound much more appetising, does it?

If her clothing allowance had run out she might have had to fashion a coat from a blanket or a pair of old curtains, and as for make-up – well, it wasn't unknown for lipstick to be replaced by beetroot juice.

And hair-spray? A mixture of sugar and water would keep that bob in place!

As the war dragged on, more and more women began to wear 'slacks', or loose trousers, with square-shouldered jackets that mimicked the cut of uniforms. A soldier would sometimes come home on leave to find that his only suit had disappeared from his wardrobe, having been turned into a costume by his fashionable sister.

Beetroot

Old curtains

Gravy browning

M avis was succeeding in her aim to become the first walking café.

And children? Many of them grew accustomed to walking about in ill-fitting hand-me-downs.

There were, remember, no washing machines in those days, so cleaning clothes meant giving them a thorough pounding in a big drum. There weren't any man-made, drip-dry materials either, so after being put through a wringer the clothes had to be hung out on the line to dry or draped on a clothes horse in front of the fire.

Yanks and nylons

American soldiers based in Britain were often regarded with envy because they seemed to have ready supplies of life's 'little extras', such as cigarettes, chewing gum and those brand new replacements for stockings, nylons.

The nylons – which first appeared in New York stores in May, 1940 – were, of course, a lure for local girls who couldn't find, or afford, the stockings they'd been accustomed to.

If you had a 'Yank' for a boyfriend you were suddenly the height of fashion!

As most families couldn't afford many spare changes of clothing it's no wonder that children would often wear the same outfit for days at a time – and be told that they mustn't carelessly make holes in it or they'd be in big, big trouble.

Make Do and Mend

And when their clothes *did* wear out? Why then it was time to rally round to the government's cry of 'Make do and mend'.

To 'make do' meant making the most of what you'd got – well, you didn't really have much choice, did you?

And to mend? This was such an effective campaign against wastage that a whole generation learned the habit of darning just about everything in sight.

'When you feel tired of your old clothes,' said the President of the Board of Trade, 'remember that by making them do you are contributing some part of an aeroplane, a gun or a tank.'

Perhaps that was some consolation to the huge army of women who now learned ingenious ways of making things last.

The government invented a figure called Mrs Sew and Sew to encourage them. (She must have annoyed them no end by keeping on about it.) Here are a few of things a real-life Mrs S and S would do:

- When her husband's shirt collars wore out she unpicked them, cut a length off the tail and re-faced the collar.

- If her son needed white shorts for sports day she cut up some old pillowcases.

- If her daughter needed a blouse she found yet more pillowcases, cut them to shape and trimmed them with lace (if she could find any).

- When a pair of woollen socks was at last beyond repair she would unravel them and mix the wool with random coloured strands from other garments to make a Fair Isle pullover.

- Once her own dress or her husband's suit were worn out she would cut them down to make clothes for her children.

- When bedroom sheets wore thin she would cut them in half, sew the sides to the middle and hem the edges.

- And she might even have time to think of herself. A fancy jacket, perhaps? Women's magazines teemed with bright ideas for making yourself look good in wartime, so she might cut up some old lace curtains to make herself 'a dashing little bolero'.

Goodness knows, she deserved a bit of glamour after all that sewing and stitching!

Help from overseas

Parcels of clothing and food were sent to Britain by individuals and organisations in America and Canada who knew how severe our shortages were.

These came over on the convoys which were carrying armaments and food across the Atlantic, and they were distributed to families who had been bombed out of their homes.

You never knew what you were going to find in the parcel, so there was a great air of excitement when it was opened.

D ennis' attempts to start the 'ripped jeans' trend were always thwarted.

Accounts of growing up during the war years are littered with rueful tales of children going out into the world dressed like scarecrows – although perhaps they didn't feel quite as embarrassed as their young counterparts would today because their friends had to suffer a similar indignity.

Wearing second-hand clothes was bearable if they (more or less) fitted, but the patches could be almost comical. When a boy's legs grew too sturdy for his trousers, for instance, his mum might well unpick the seams and insert some extra material to give him more room. If the new material matched he was lucky: all too often it would be of a completely different colour.

One lad later remembered the day his parents bought him a 'horrible' pair of heavy, hobnailed first world war boots from a man selling government surplus material from a horse and cart.

He was very embarrassed when he first wore them to school, but to his amazement they were all the rage: all the boys wanted a pair!

A nation of knits

Local authorities organised special 'Make do and Mend' classes for women who had never learned the necessary skills before.

A slogan seen on hoardings everywhere read, 'If you can knit – you can do your bit.'

Women's Institutes and other organisations did *their* bit by holding knitting circles, following special 'War Knitting' patterns.

There were 'Make do and Mend' weeks, when exhibitions were held to show how to re-feet knitted socks, knit patches for worn out jumper elbows and let dresses down – hiding the worn hemline with coloured braid.

Talk to the older generation and you'll hear countless yarns (sorry!) about unravelling old cardigans and socks in order to use the wool all over again to make new ones. The clicking never stopped.

In fact, knitting had suddenly become a national obsession.

MAKE-DO AND MEND

says Mrs Sew-and-Sew

This was also her attitude towards her husband.

The Sirdar Wool Company produced wool especially dyed in service colours (Navy blue, Air Force blue and grey and Army khaki) and the industrious volunteers set about making pullovers, socks, gloves and scarves for the armed forces.

There were specialised patterns to suit particular operations – a balaclava helmet with ear flaps for use in telephone operations, for instance, a knitted helmet cap to provide warmth under a soldier's metal helmet and mittens that exposed the forefinger with which a marksman pulled the trigger.

Time would be set aside at school for knitting sessions, during which both girls and boys would make more straightforward garments. They would often send them to particular regiments or to individual ships and would receive 'thank you' letters in return.

The sad downside of this was the children occasionally learned that the sailors for whom they had been busy knitting jumpers had gone down with their ship in the Atlantic. That really brought home the reality of war.

Salvage

The campaign to save and re-use materials extended well beyond fabric and clothing.

Here are a few of the things the government was keen to collect:

- Waste paper.
- Rags.
- Bones.
- Pots and pans.

You may wonder what on earth these could be used for, but they did make a difference to the war effort. The paper and rags were reprocessed – 'recycled' we'd say today – while the bones were turned into glue for aircraft manufacture.

As for the pots and pans, their aluminium was to be used to make the Spitfires which played such a vital role against the German Luftwaffe during the Battle of Britain.

Calling all handymen

The war years were a great time for do-it-yourself enthusiasts – if they had the time, of course.

After all, the great challenge was to make the most of the few materials at your disposal, and some men loved rising to it.

In 1940 Batsford published *101 Things to do in Wartime,* which covered toy-making (*see page 131*), knitting projects, cookery, first aid and creating cases for gas masks, among much else.

One section with a Make Do and Mend theme was headed 'Using Up Scraps of Metal and Wood'.

Here are a few of the things that could be made 'for home use or as acceptable presents' with the use of 'some ingenuity and ordinary care':

- **A match-box rack.** ('Generally welcomed by the housewife.')

- **A spring for use as a paper clip.**

- **Corner clips for a blotting pad.**

Life could be very exciting on the Home Front!

The scheme was the brainchild of Lord Beaverbrook, the *Daily Express* newspaper tycoon, who came up with all sorts of ideas like this – including a fund-raising scheme which set the cost of a Spitfire at a notional £5,000, although it was really more than twice that.

The public responded enthusiastically to the call to empty their kitchens and sheds of surplus gadgets, and soon the salvage dumps were full to overflowing with everything from pots, pans and kettles to tin baths and cigarette boxes.

Over twenty different types of Spitfire were built during the war, including a navy version called the Seafire.

Spitfire Mark Vb

Aluminium milk bottle tops were also in great demand, and children were encouraged to take them into their schools by the hundreds.

One lad, who admitted to wondering how many tops it would take to make a Spitfire, later recalled that an unofficial rank was bestowed on collectors by his headmaster.

You would become a corporal if you took in a hundred of them, while 500 would make you a lieutenant, and so on – but he was discouraged when another lad became a field marshall almost overnight!

Any old iron

Ships and tanks required tougher metals, and many thousands of tons of decorative ironwork and railings were sliced up and carried away from parks, gardens and the street fronts of buildings in the towns.

It was later claimed that this scheme was dreamed up as much to improve public morale as to create more tanks. It encouraged the feeling that everyone was working together.

If, as is now generally accepted, little of the cast iron was used in the war effort, what happened to it?

Well, there are several unconfirmed accounts of it being dumped – in the River Severn, in the sea a mile off the coast of Bognor Regis and in the Thames estuary. London dockers later added the colourful detail that ships needed pilots to guide them through because their compasses were badly affected by passing over so much iron on the sea-bed.

Meanwhile, in Singapore...

After the Japanese overran the British colony of Singapore in 1942 they swiftly ransacked private and public buildings for as much scrap metal as they could find.

In most cases they took the obvious things, including the railings around churches and (worryingly) the security bars protecting house windows.

More surprising was their removal of the iron posts which carried the power supply for the local trams – which of course stopped running.

What's certainly true is that many towns were disfigured by the dismantling of their ironwork, and that some still display the sorry stumps of former gates and railings.

Can you find any near you?

The Squander Bug

The government's campaign against waste used a grim looking character called the Squander Bug, who was a dirty yellow colour and covered with German swastikas.

One poster read. 'Don't take the Squander Bug when you go shopping'. Four cartoon boxes with bubble captions begin with a woman telling a friend that she's 'doing a bit of shopping this afternoon'.

The Squander Bug ('This is where I come in') beckons her into a store, saying 'Spend it here – prices are fantastic.'

She comes out with her purchase, thinking 'I don't suppose it's worth half the money,' to which the Squander Bug adds with a huge, triumphant laugh, 'And it doesn't help the war a bit.'

It must have been a bit tiresome being lectured like this all the time, but you were nagged about nearly everything in wartime.

Your clothes were threadbare, your diet was boring, and yet you were made to feel guilty even when you jumped on a bus!

Like fuel, petrol
coupons could run
out at any time.

CHAPTER fOUR

AND A fEW OTHER THINGS...

Petrol, imported from overseas, was the very first thing to be rationed – within a few weeks of the outbreak of war.

It was vital that the little fuel we had should be used by the armed forces and for essential work on the farms and in industry, so it's surprising that private motorists (there were far fewer then, of course) were at first given ration books and allowed a small amount for ordinary use.

This later changed, and 'pleasure motoring' was off the agenda.

Before the war, as now, various companies (Shell, Esso and so on) competed to sell petrol to motorists, but the Secretary for Mines, Geoffrey Lloyd, put an immediate stop to that.

'Petrol distributors throughout the country,' he announced in September 1939, 'have arranged to pool all their resources and, after the individual brands still in stock at garages and service stations have been sold by them at the prices now ruling, one grade only of motor spirit will be supplied to the public.

Coloured fuel

Tractors and commercial vehicles were given an allowance of special 'leaded' petrol not available to private motorists, and it was coloured red to distinguish it from the rest.

People who wanted to cheat the system and use it in their own cars tried various methods of getting rid of the colour, including putting 'black lead' into it and straining it through women's silk stockings.

It was risky though: if they were caught they faced a heavy fine.

'This spirit will be called "pool" motor spirit and will be on sale ex-pump in England and Wales at 1s 6d per gallon.'

There was an alternative, though – coal gas – and vehicles didn't need much tinkering with in order to be able to use it. (A mixing valve had to be connected to the carburettor – don't try it at home!)

As early as September 21st the *Daily Telegraph* reported an initiative in the north of England:

The Bradford municipal gas undertaking is to open eight filling stations to supply motorists with coal gas as an alternative to petrol.

Containers for the fuel are in the form of either canvas bags carried on the roof or metal cylinders in which the gas is charged under pressure.

Portable gas-producing plants for industrial and commercial vehicles are being produced by several firms. On the Continent, where they were in the main developed, they use charcoal or wood as fuel. In this country the chief fuel is anthracite.

The cost of a plant is from about £70 upward, with an additional charge for fitting and conversion of the existing engine.

A considerable saving in fuel costs over petrol or even diesel oil is claimed.

Cars and buses looked rather comical with these large bags and cylinders perched on top, and vehicles which carried one of the portable plants in their boot were chuggy, smelly and left a tell-tale trail of cinders in their wake.

There were no new cars on the roads, of course. The plants which made them were now given over to producing aircraft, tanks or other vehicles that were needed for the war effort.

Since many tradesmen still used horses and carts in those days, there wasn't a great disruption to supplies for most people, but if you lived miles out in the country the usual tradesman's van might begin to make less frequent trips in your direction.

This isn't to say that some farmers with a special supply of fuel for their vital work on the land always kept strictly within the rules. If they wanted an evening in town to visit the local public houses, some of them weren't above loading their truck with sacks to make their trip appear legitimate.

Life on two wheels

The bicycle came into its own during the second world war. Almost everyone seemed to have one, and people became accustomed to taking what we would today regard as incredibly long journeys on them, both for work and pleasure.

Although most other factories concentrated on war work, bicycles were still being made by British manufacturers such as BSA, Raleigh, Dawes and Claude Butler.

Cyclists almost had the roads to themselves because of petrol rationing. During the blackout they were supposed to have dimmed lights at the front and the back. Some daredevil youngsters risked a fine by not bothering – knowing that, with fit police officers serving in the army, they could easily outpace the older constables who huffed and puffed as they tried to catch them.

You'd think that the roads would have been much safer with nothing much on them but buses, commercial vehicles, ambulances and the like, but at night a strict blackout was imposed. Even though a 20mph speed limit was introduced, the accident rate soared because people careered into things.

Meanwhile, in America...

Why was petrol rationing introduced in America during the war? After all, there were huge oilfields beneath the ground in Texas.

The United States suffered a shortage not in oil but rubber, which had previously come from countries in the Far East now occupied by the Japanese.

The government imposed a ban on buying rubber goods, including beach balls, hot-water bottles, garden hoses – and car tyres. The petrol rationing was to save the tyres.

Shanks' pony

As motorists left their cars in the garage, there was an increasing pressure on public transport, and the government began a campaign discouraging people from using it when they didn't have to. They were advised to use 'Shanks' pony' (meaning their own two legs), and there were posters which read 'Walk short distances and leave room for those who have longer journeys'. There was, of course, a verse to go with it, the idea being to heap shame upon the head of the 'transport hog':

You wonder why we make a fuss
If George decides to take a bus,
But look again and you will see
That George ain't all that George should be.
He's only got a step to go –
A couple hundred yards or so –
While others further down the queue
Have far to go and lots to do.
When George gets on we often find
That other folk get left behind.
He pays his fare and rides the stage
And off he hops – and see the rage!
And seeing this gives George a jog:
'Perhaps I'm just a Transport Hog.'

Yarooh – no comics!

The over-sized Billy Bunter of Greyfriars School was among the most notable victims of wartime scarcity.

During what became known as 'the graveyard week' (May 18th–25th, 1940) the *Magnet* and a whole sheaf of children's comics closed down because paper was so scarce.

Many of them never appeared again – although Bunter, who had featured in no fewer than 1,670 issues of the *Magnet*, proved to be irrepressible, eating his way through mountains of food in the post-war novels and television plays of his author, Frank Richards.

Why the shortage? It's the same old story. Books and newspapers weren't made from sturdy English oaks and elms but from the fast-growing conifers grown in much greater quantities overseas. Our supplies were cut off.

Most of the few comics which survived came out fortnightly rather than weekly, and their quality inevitably suffered. The paper was poorer, and the colour was weaker.

Newspapers were in great demand by readers hungry for news of the war (they eagerly pored over maps of battles on the various war fronts), but they were similarly only shadows of their former selves.

They were very thin – sometimes a single folded sheet making four pages – and there was very little advertising in them (what was there to sell?) apart from government advice on avoiding waste, 'making do' and taking care not to pass information to the enemy: 'Careless talk costs lives'.

As for books, they continued to appear, but they were severely reduced in size and length, and smaller type faces were used in an attempt to cram as much information as possible into a small space. Ambitious works would have to be put on hold for years.

Six publish Enid's books

The children's author Enid Blyton managed to persuade the authorities that she had too many staff and that her writing privacy was too important for her to house young evacuees.

She also managed to keep publishing at a phenomenal rate (she wrote about 185 novels in her lifetime and more than 4,000 short stories) despite the wartime paper shortages.

An individual publishing house would have had trouble finding enough paper to cope, so she used 'lashings' of them – six in all.

Precious bags

This was a time before the plastic bags and shrink-wrapped packaging we take for granted today, and suddenly the humble paper variety became something to hang on to. You'd take one with you when you went shopping, and when you got home and emptied it you might iron it flat to make sure you could use it again the next day. Yes, things were that desperate!

A youngster sent to buy fish and chips would get a withering look from behind the counter if she hadn't taken wrapping paper with her. If she *was* given some, it would probably be a single sheet and her hands would be burning by the time she got home.

Back to Dickens

The idea of using slates rather than exercise books in the classroom sounds Dickensian, but there are many memories of that from the war. (Presumably the schools dug them out from the depths of a cupboard somewhere.) For some it was back to chalk and a duster, while others made letters on slates with wooden borders filled with sand. They traced them with their fingers, carried them gingerly to their teacher and then shook the sand level to start all over again.

Those who *did* have books to write in had to use up every last inch of space before they would be given a new one. Many of them grew up to become the folk you know today, who save every bit of spare paper and insist on writing on both sides of it.

Meanwhile, in New Zealand...

Paper shortages weren't exclusive to Britain, and in New Zealand the government's drive against wastage encouraged people to use both sides of every sheet they used.

Unhappily, the campaign got off to a bad start. It involved creating large posters, which was seen as a terrible waste of paper – especially as they were only printed on one side!

Something to sit on

The timber shortage also affected furniture manufacture at a time when literally millions of people needed to replace beds, chairs and wardrobes destroyed during German bombing raids.

Consider a few striking figures from the London Blitz alone – and they relate only to the most severe period of bombing between 7 Sepember 1940 and 11 May, 1941:

- 40,000 civilians killed.
- 46,000 seriously injured.
- 1,000,000 houses destroyed or badly damaged.

And now here's a list of the mayhem suffered in just a few other cities:

- **Liverpool** – 1,453 people were killed, 4,400 houses destroyed and 51,000 people made homeless in a single week during May 1941.

- **Hull** – of the 92,660 houses standing before the Blitz fewer than 6,000 survived unscathed, 1,200 people were killed and 152,000 were made homeless.

• Sheffield – Over just two December nights in 1941 600 people were killed, 1,500 were injured and 40,000 were made homeless.

• Coventry – In a single devastating raid on 14 November 1940 568 people were killed, 1,200 were seriously injured and 43,000 houses were destroyed.

• Exeter – During 19 attacks throughout the war 265 people were killed and 1,809 homes were destroyed.

Utility furniture

As the survivors attempted to rebuild their lives, usually in temporary accommodation, the government was determined that they shouldn't be the victims of manufacturers out to make an indecent profit from their misery.

It was also clear that, since there was a severe shortage of wood and other materials, the new furniture would have to be pretty basic.

This is how 'utility furniture' was born – using economical materials to create a small range of state-approved designs at fixed prices.

Back to Basics

Utility furniture could be bought by those regarded as most in need of it – principally people bombed out of their houses, couples who had just got married and children who had grown out of their existing beds .

They were given coupons: a maximum 60 units for a couple and 10 for each child in the family.

You had to choose carefully, because the coupons certainly wouldn't kit out a palace. Here's what some of the 30 articles in the scheme were worth:

Wardrobe (4ft)	12 units
Wardrobe (3ft)	10 units
Bedsettee	10 units
Chest of drawers	8 units
Kitchen cabinet	8 units
Sideboard	8 units
Kitchen table (large)	6 units
Kitchen table (small)	4 units
Armchair	6 units
Fireside chair	5 units
Metal bedstead	5 units
Shelves	3 units
Dining chair	1 unit

These items had to be paid for, of course, and the prices ranged from £1.9s for a dining chair to £10.7s for a wardrobe.

The idea was to make these designs so simple that the furniture could be mass-produced by a wide range of woodworking businesses – not all of them having furniture-making skills.

And it was important that these should be as local as possible to the people who needed the stuff, because you didn't want the nation criss-crossed by lorries during a petrol shortage.

In the end there were as many as 700 firms producing furniture with the official CC41 utility mark etched on it (as with utility clothing). This mark was commonly known as 'the cheeses' as the 'C's looked like two wheels of cheese.

You won't be surprised to learn that people were somewhat sniffy about what was on offer. After all, the backs of the wardrobes were made of hardboard ('cardboard' they called it), and so were the bases of the drawers. Everything was extremely plain, and the backs of chairs were lower than their pre-war counterparts to save wood. True, there was no ban on buying non-utility furniture – but that was expensive.

R osemary had always
dreamt of hardboard
kitchen units.

Rules and regulations

To give you an idea of the hoops people had to jump through to survive in wartime, here's an edited version of a Board of Trade document about getting hold of utility furniture. It sounds very bossy – but perhaps it had to be.

- Production is limited and the demand is heavy and increasing. In order that everyone who is eligible may get his fair share no applicant is allowed more than a maximum number of units varying according to the size of his family. No allowance can be made for lodgers and visitors.

- Couples who are not furnishing a home of their own but have to furnish their own bedroom are given units for bedroom furniture only. The maximum allowance is 25 units (sufficient for a double bed, a large size wardrobe and tallboy or large size dressing chest) with a small addition for each child.

- If the applicant already has some furniture available for his use, or where built in furniture is provided in pre fabricated houses or temporary bungalows, the maximum allowance is reduced accordingly.

- Bedsettees and divans are more expensive in labour and materials than beds, and units cannot be allowed for them where a bed would meet the need.

- You are free to use your units to buy what furniture you choose but you should take care to include in your order the articles you need most urgently. No extra units will be granted if you fail to order something essential nor will deferred units be exchanged for current ones.

- It is illegal to sell permits or units or to give or transfer them to anyone else. If the need for which you are given a permit does not arise (e.g. if you do not set up a house after all) you must return it.

- If you buy second hand utility furniture the shopkeeper must collect the full number of units. The instructions given on the permit and in this leaflet apply to all utility furniture, but not to non-utility furniture which you can buy without a permit.

- Utility nursery furniture (that is cots, playpens and babies' chairs) can be bought without a permit, but there will only be enough for people who really need it and you should not buy a new chair or cot if you have an old one which will do.

The irony is that these utility chairs, tables and wardrobes later became collectors' items. No, they weren't made to last, and yes, the materials were cheap, but they had a distinctive 'modern' design. Much of the credit for this is due to Gordon Russell, the furniture manufacturer who was put in charge of the government's utility furniture advisory committee. He saw the scheme as a great chance break from what he saw as the fussy, pseudo-Victorian tradition which was still in vogue before the war.

An excuse to be dirty

Young lads are said to have rejoiced in February 1942 when soap was put on the ration in order to save oils and fats for food.

Most people were allowed four coupons each month, although there were concessions for babies, invalids and some workers.

Each of the following used up one coupon: 4oz (113 gm) bar hard soap; 3oz (85gm) bar toilet soap; ½oz (14gm) liquid soap; 6oz (170gm) soft soap; 3oz (i5gm) soap flakes; 6oz (170gm) soap powder.

Of course there would later be a reaction against this 'honest', unadorned style, but it did have a lasting effect. Take a look around you today!

A burning problem

Britain still had plenty of coal mines when the war broke out, but the country nevertheless soon found itself short of the stuff.

This was partly because so many of the miners were called up to serve in the armed forces (as many as 36,000 of them), and when the call went out for other men to replace them the response was far from enthusiastic.

Is that surprising? Descending hundreds of feet into the depths of the earth to hack away at coal in cramped tunnels would be hell for most of us, and the mines relied on men whose families had toiled away at it for generations.

Making your own fuel

Here's some advice from the book *101 Things to Do in War Time*, written by Lillie B. and Arthur C. Horth and published by Batsford in 1940:

- Coal fires can be kept going by using coke, and when not required to give out a lot of heat they can be banked down with coal dust.

- All the coal dust in the cellar or bin should be piled up on one side and kept for this purpose or made into briquettes. The latter can be made by mixing together one part of coal tar pitch to nine parts of coal dust, heated over a fire.

- The mixture can be poured into moulds formed by cardboard boxes. If clay is available, use the same proportions, but in this case the mixture can be moulded into balls and left to dry.

- Prepared coal in the form of Coalite is economical, and it will be found that the installation of an anthracite stove will give continuous heat at a lower cost than a large open fire.

In July 1941 coal went 'on the ration', with households limited to a hundredweight a week for fifty weeks. Unless they were going to scrabble around for offcuts of wood for the remaining two weeks they would just have to keep some by, but saving fuel for bitterly cold periods was advisable in any case.

In those days a great many homes relied on coal fires for their heating and coal-fired ranges for their cooking, so people felt the cutbacks pretty deeply. The substitute 'briquettes' (made of compressed coal dust) were regarded as distinctly second-rate, being hard to light and inclined to 'spit'.

A better bet was coke, a smokeless fuel that was rather easier to find than coal. Indeed, the government encouraged people to use it, with an advertising campaign whose slogan was 'Get the coke habit!'

Bevin Boys

In 1943, with the situation becoming desperate (planned power cuts in the home were commonplace because the power stations were low on coal) the Minister of Labour, Ernest Bevin, decided to force young men into the mines, through a kind of lottery involving all those between 18 and 25 who hadn't yet enlisted in the armed forces. One of his secretaries would pick a number from a hat each week, and all new recruits who had that digit at the end of their National Service number were added to the list of trainee miners.

This must have been a shock to young men dreaming of glory in a cockpit or out on the ocean waves, and 40 per cent of those whose name came up asked not to do it. A few hundred of them did have their appeals allowed, but the rest had to go down the mines or into prison – as 147 chose to do. In the end some 21,800 served as so-called 'Bevin Boys' alongside another 16,000 young men who had opted for coal mining when first called up.

Ten Bevin Boys

1. **Peter Archer** Now Lord Archer of Sandwell; a former MP and solicitor general for England and Wales from 1974–1979.

2. **Stanley Bailey** Former chief constable of Northumbria Police.

3. **John Comer** English actor, perhaps best known as the cafe owner during the first ten years of *Last of the Summer Wine*.

4. **Paul Hamlyn** Now Lord Hamlyn, the founder of the Hamlyn publishing group and the Music for Pleasure record label.

5. **Eric Morecambe** One half of the famous British comedy duo, Morecambe and Wise.

6. **Jock Purdon** Folk singer and poet, who stayed on in the mines after the war.

7. **Brian Rix** Actor/manager, now Lord Rix and president of the Mencap charity.

8. **Nat Lofthouse** England international footballer.

9. **Alf Sherwood** Wales international footballer.

10. **Peter Shaffer** Dramatist who wrote the plays *Equus* and *Amadeus*.

Dying for a fag

Smoking was much more widespread during the war years than it is today, and many people were unaware of how dangerous it was for their health.

Cigarettes and tobacco weren't rationed, but they were in short supply, and there were long queues outside the shops when a shipment came in.

If they couldn't buy their 'fags' legitimately, many people addicted to them would pay much more than the going price to anyone who could produce them.

As we've seen, some gardeners tried growing tobacco in their 'dig for victory' plots. Other desperate smokers would pick and dry herbs for their 'roll ups' or pipes as a substitute.

Alas, the colourful 'cigarette cards' inserted in each packet were a victim of the paper shortage. These were produced as sets – footballers, birds, national flags and so on – and children loved collecting them.

Something to do

Toys and games were an inevitable casualty of wartime shortages. They weren't rationed, but the materials to make them were hard to get – and nobody (except for the children who wanted a bit of harmless fun among all the shock and horror around them) regarded them as a priority.

Don't forget that there were none of the electronic gizmos that we enjoy today, and that even before the war the younger generation generally had far less spent on them, and very little to spend on themselves. The smaller ones, if a member of their family was a handyman, might get a small wooden toy, and (remember the sound of those click-clacking needles?) knitted gifts would almost be coming of your ears at Christmas. You'd have a knitted stocking and you couldn't even expect to find an orange in it!

The unluckier ones might even be given a knitted swimsuit, guaranteed to cause maximum embarrassment when the time came to clamber, heavily dripping, from the pool. Those who enjoyed putting their nose into a book or a comic could learn to make do with the limited publications on offer, but it became very difficult during dark winter evenings when the blackout was in force and the light in your home or shelter was horribly dim.

The same applied to playing outside, even if there was no bombing raid that night. In effect, light was rationed – and chasing a football in the pitch darkness was likely to give you a bloody nose from running smack into a wall.

Here are a few of the common games and pastimes enjoyed and endured during the war:

- Cards
- Indoor games such as Monopoly, Ludo and Tiddlywinks
- Jigsaw puzzles
- Skipping
- Chasing games
- Hide and seek
- Marbles
- Spinning tops
- Hoops

M
ichael was grateful to
Auntie Margaret for
his knitted football.

Sport in wartime

For youngsters who enjoyed being taken to professional sports events the war was an awful nuisance!

Football was the nation's favourite game, but most of the players had been 'called up' to join the armed forces. That didn't mean there were no games at all to watch, but you couldn't expect to see your favourite stars, and the chances were that the teams who turned up would be a mixture of amateurs and professionals.

The cheaply produced, single-sheet programme would sometimes have 'A.N. Other' listed as one of the players, because the club itself wouldn't know who to expect in its line-up. The main thing was to have a match to put on.

The Football League programme was abandoned at the outbreak of war, and matches were organised on a regional basis. In London, Arsenal had to share the nearby ground of their great rivals Tottenham Hotspur because their Highbury Stadium was taken over by the military.

Cricket was similarly affected. Lord's cricket ground was requisitioned by the War Office (used by the RAF).

In 1940 a 1000lb German bomb came down in the outfield at the Nursery End at Lord's: it failed to explode, but left a huge crater.

The country cricket championship was abandoned until 1946, but the MCC (Marylebone Cricket Club) did arrange one-day matches throughout the war, with the profits made from ticket sales being given to charities such as the Red Cross.

Rugby was also played on an informal basis, and it clearly operated on the proverbial shoe-string. One Scottish player won his first cap shortly before leaving to fight in the war. When he was picked again six years later the authorities expected him to have his original shirt in his sports bag!

What all children seem to have been given was plenty of well-meaning advice about how to enjoy themselves, and there was no end of books with titles such as *101 Things for Girls to Do*, *101 Things for Boys to Make* (note the subtle difference) and *101 Things for Little Folks to Do*.

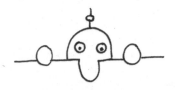

Shrapnel hunting

When you woke up in a British city during the Blitz you were likely to find the world outside your shelter looking rather different from how you last saw it.

Children were as much affected by the horrors of war as anyone else, but they did get a thrill from searching among the wreckage for pieces of shrapnel (fragments of exploded shells) and other memorabilia.

A piece from a crashed aeroplane was even more prized, and youngsters would eagerly make 'swaps' to improve their collections.

A fold-out booklet published by the Nursery School Association was called *Toys from Tins*, and it included all kinds of bright ideas for fashioning items from materials you might otherwise have thrown away or – more likely, perhaps – donated to the war effort.

You could, with ingenuity, create a complete tin train set from an old coffee pot, sardine and boot polish tins, an array of cotton reels, some offcuts of wood and an assortment of nails, screws and washers.

The book even told you how to make the surrounding landscape, with cows (more cotton reels, plus wire for heads and tails and leather scraps for ears) and trees (teasel heads and pine cones).

More strange ways to get by

All sorts of things were hard to get during the war, but alternatives were at hand – not all of them recommended:

- **Cleaning pots and pans.** Crush eggshells to use as a scouring compound.

- **Scrubbing woodwork.** Use the dregs of cold tea.

- **Cleaning your teeth.** No toothpaste? Use salt or soot, or a combination of both. (Really!)

- **Washing clothes.** Boil scraps of soap, let them cool and then use a cheese grater to make soap flakes.

- **Baby's cot.** Can't afford to buy one? Find an old drawer and line it with curtain material. (Sleep tight, little one!)

- **Suffering from head lice?** Soak your hair in paraffin and later wash the nits out with vinegar water.

- **Can't get chewing gum?** Soften up a lump of candle wax and flavour it with shavings from an Oxo cube. (Don't swallow it!)

Just making it would keep you busy for days. When you'd finished that, you could get to work on 'tins for waterplay', a set of nine pins, a scooter or a steam roller.

It might not be perfect, but you could bet there wouldn't be another one quite like it anywhere in the neighbourhood...

No, it wasn't easy either for adults or for children during the last war – but some people couldn't resist the opportunity of making a profit at other people's expense, as we'll see in the next chapter.

from smugglers to spivs

It's a fact of human nature that whenever there are shortages there will be those who seek to make a large profit from supplying other people's needs.

In times gone by they were known as smugglers. During the 18th and 19th centuries the government imposed taxes on a wide range of goods, including brandy, tea and tobacco, and that prompted the 'free traders' to bring them ashore on dark, moonless nights – in order to avoid the taxes.

In the United States of America, during the 1920s and early 1930s, they were known as bootleggers. The government had banned the sale of alcohol, and this meant that there was a lot of money to be made by making it, or importing it, illegally.

During the second world war in Britain they were known as spivs. These were the 'wide boys' (another frequently used term) who would trade in rationed goods, charging prices well above those fixed by the government.

CHAPTER five

THE BLACK MARKET

AND OTHER fIDDLES

t would be good to believe that the wartime spirit made everyone work together for the common good, with no room for callous selfishness.

No such luck!

There were, indeed, countless acts of heroism during these years, and most people did strive to lend a hand to others and make the best of their terrible circumstances.

Unhappily, these very cirumstances made it possible for the unscrupulous to make a 'killing' from their neighbours' sufferings.

The blackout offered an obvious opportunity to thieves who could break into shops and houses and ransack bombed buildings with less chance of being caught.

Many *were* caught, though: during the first two months of the Blitz nearly 400 people were taken to court for looting. The Mayor of London said it should be a hanging offence, and others agreed with him, although the courts stopped far short of that.

It was a particularly nasty blow to learn that some of the culprits were those whose duty it was to help the victims, such as policemen and fire-fighters. Indeed, of the first twenty cases heard at the Old Bailey in London on 9th November 1940, ten involved members of the auxiliary fire service.

In Sheffield looters operated on a wholesale scale, and a judge in Leeds spoke of 'two men who had abandoned well-paid positions, one of them earning £7 to £9 a week, and work of public importance, and who abandoned it to take up the obviously more remunerative occupation of looting'.

How to break the law

Introducing new rules to create fairness was generally regarded as a good idea, but before long the government had created so much new legislation (not all of it connected with rationing) that many people grew resentful.

Of course you weren't allowed to buy and sell rationed goods except with coupons and at the fixed prices, but here are a few of the other things you couldn't do:

- Strike a match in the street during the blackout.
- Visit the seaside unless you had written permission to enter what was at the time, a restricted area.
- Rear more pigs than agreed with the authorities.
- If you were a housewife, hoard more than one week's supply of food in your larder.
- If you were a tradesman, waste petrol by deviating more than 800 yards from your allotted route.
- If you were a restaurateur, serve both meat and fish to a customer during a single meal.
- If you were a florist, send cut flowers by train to London, in contravention of The Transportation of Flowers Order.
- If you were the owner of a public house, decorate your premises without a licence.

In Dover, after a heavy air raid during which several houses had been destroyed in a single street, looters systematically picked their way through them all, carrying away everything they could find.

'Carpets have been stripped from the floors,' a local chief inspector reported. 'Stair carpets have been removed – they have even taken away heavy mangles, bedsteads and complete suites of furniture.'

Meanwhile in Russia...

People can get used to shortages of most things, but if they have an addiction they will often pay excessive amounts to feed their habit. Tobacco was rationed in Russia during the war, and black marketeers immediately moved in to make a killing.

Amazingly, they didn't need to sell the tobacco in order to cash in. They would stand on street corners with lit cigarettes and charge passers-by two roubles for every puff they took.

Whatever you do, try not to think about the health implications!

Also in Kent, a group of army deserters went on a rampage of looting and were given sentences ranging from five years in gaol to eight years hard labour.

Guns, too

More worrying were the frequent thefts of weapons and ammunition from Home Guard armaments stores. In March 1943 three 17-year-olds youths held up the cashier at the Ambassador cinema in Hayes, London, with three loaded sten-guns that had been stolen from the local Home Guard store. After they were arrested they admitted that they had taken part in 43 other raids in London.

There were many cases of large-scale theft and fraud. Gangs, often with inside help, would raid depots supplying military canteens and shops (belonging to the NAAFI, or Navy, Army and Air Force Institute) and would sell the food and other stolen goods on the black market. It was against the law to buy rationed goods without coupons, but the temptation was too great for many people. They happily paid up.

The open air market in Romford, Essex, was notorious for its black market trade. 'Tic tac men' (just like those on race courses) would send hand signals to one another to warn of a police raid.

Here food would openly be sold without coupons, while new clothes would be marked 'second-hand' or 'shop-soiled', which allowed them to be traded without coupons as long as they cost no more than £2.12s.

Undercover inspectors had just begun to get control of the situation when 100,000 ration books (worth more than £500,000) were stolen from the local Ministry of Food offices. These very soon appeared at the market in the hands of customers now able to buy 'legally'.

"And these would really give your vehicle a bit of class."

Some big names caught in the net

It wasn't only the man or woman in the street who were caught breaking the law in wartime. Some well-known figures appeared in court:

- **Noel Coward.** The famous dramatist, song writer and entertainer was fined for committing a minor currency offence, and Winston Churchill denied him a knighthood because of it. (It came his way years later.)

- **Ivor Novello.** The famous composer and actor was sent to prison for eight weeks after fraudulently obtaining petrol for his Rolls-Royce. Apparently it was supplied to him by a female admirer, who got it from her boss.

- **Major-General Sir Percy Laurie.** The Provost Marshal (the officer in charge of the military police) was found guilty of illegally possessing a second ration book. He told the court he thought he was entitled to have one for Great Britain and another while abroad.

- **Sir William Jowitt.** The solicitor general (one of the leading law officers in the land) appeared in court for supplying animal food without coupons to his farm in Kent. He said that he had 'not the smallest knowledge' that rules were being broken – and as he was seen as someone of 'the highest respectability', the prosecution decided not to ask for a conviction. Lucky man!

A heavy hand

While few people condoned this sort of thing (not publicly, anyway), there was a growing feeling that the authorities were going 'over the top' – bringing charges against people who had either committed a minor infringement of the law or had simply made a mistake. There seemed to be no common sense.

Someone, for instance, was given a month in prison for allowing light to escape from behind a curtain, while a rescue worker who, at the end of an exhausting day, took a swig from a near-empty bottle of gin he had picked up from the wreckage of a bombed house, found himself in court accused of looting, just as if he had loaded the victims' furniture into a van.

Here are a few other 'crimes' for which people were fined:

- Taking vegetables from a waste bin.
- Stealing an onion from an allotment.
- Wasting electricity by leaving a light on.
- Picking apples from a tree.

We've heard the story of the doctor who sold portions of an 'illegal' pig to his patients (*see page 75*), and this kind of petty crime – as it had now become – was common enough, however guilty people sometimes felt about it.

Here are a few of the countless stories told of buying on the black market:

• The father who came home with his face bloody after being caught out in a bombing raid, but who hadn't been to the hospital because he feared being given a fine: he'd bought two eggs illegally for his children and the smashed evidence lay in his soggy pocket.

• The woman who was given black market coupons and then had her handbag stolen: she was terrified that the police would find it with the coupons inside, but luckily the thief took the coupons before discarding the bag.

• The mother and daughter who bought a piglet at a farm and took it home on a bus wrapped in a shawl, only for a police officer to sit down on the next seat: it was the most uncomfortable journey of their lives.

Insider dealing

When the food control officer in Brighton discovered that 80,000 ration books had been stolen from the local food office based in the Royal Pavilion, the police decided to use a plain clothes officer to go 'under cover' and buy some.

This proved successful, and the gang was soon caught. Imagine the shock, however, when it emerged that their ring-leader was the very enforcement officer at the Pavilion who had first reported the theft. She was imprisoned for three years.

Brighton Royal Pavilion

Meanwhile, in Poland...

Hitler had spoken of his desire to kill 'without pity or mercy, all men, women and children of Polish descent or language,' and the Polish people were reduced to effective slavery after the German invasion in 1939. Six million died, half of them Polish Jews, who were denied all human rights and sent to the death camps.

Although the country was agriculturally rich, severe rationing was introduced so that the occupying army ate well while those labourers it needed to work in the mines and the factories were fed just enough to survive. Nobody else mattered.

In the cities millions of people faced starvation – and it was the black market which saved them. Peasant growers or their 'middle men' travelled for many miles under cover of darkness (on foot or by horse and cart) in the knowledge that they were likely to be shot on the spot if caught breaking the regulations.

Other black marketeers arrived by train, carrying seemingly innocent brief cases packed with red meat.

Their motives were no doubt mixed. Some of them made huge profits, taking advantage of their customers' desperation. Without them, though, the appalling suffering in the cities would have been even worse than it was.

• The butcher's boy who would regularly take a disguised ham to the baker and bring home 'indigestion powder' – highly valued sugar.

• The little girl who watched as a local man who sold black market silk underwear from a suitcase was chased by the police: her respectable grandma hid the case 'because everyone stuck together in those days'.

• The blameless auntie who, with a finger to her lips, produced a tin of clotted cream from under the dustbin after the local dairyman had delivered the milk. In these circumstances questions simply weren't asked.

All of these people were taking a risk, because the law was often strictly enforced. Parliament passed legislation which enabled the courts to impose fines of up to £500, with or without two years' imprisonment, plus three times the sum involved.

Sneaks and Snoopers

Meanwhile, at the Odeon Theatre in Streatham, Surrey, the manageress and two of her waitresses were fined for 'aiding and abetting' the serving of both meat and fish to a customer.

And who was the customer? Why, an assistant enforcement officer, who knew very well when he ordered the food that he was encouraging staff to break the law!

Here was a nasty side to law enforcement. It was bad enough that members of the public would sometimes inform the authorities if they knew of a trader who was bending the rules. People didn't like sneaks.

But now it became obvious that the authorities were acting as 'agents provocateurs' – that is, pretending to be genuine customers in order to provoke shopkeepers and restaurateurs into wrong-doing. That kind of snooping was widely condemned in the newspapers.

How did they go about it?

In December 1940, Stepney council in the East End of London employed a woman to visit butchers' shops and try to buy meat without coupons. Three of them in a single road found themselves heavily fined for it – which no doubt acted as a warning to others.

That was straightforward. A much more cunning approach was used in the London borough of Hendon. This involved a team of women who hoped to trick shop assistants into selling them goods without coupons.

The 'customer' would hand over her ration book and ask for two ounces of tea. Just as the shop assistant had almost finished serving her she would change her mind and ask for four ounces. If the assistant forgot to take out a second two-ounce coupon she would be charged with breaking the rationing restrictions.

In no time at all some 59 Hendon shopkeepers had been successfully prosecuted for the offence.

Caught in the act

From *The East Grinstead Observer*,
28th August, 1943:

"A well-known East Grinstead resident, Bernard Richardson, of Half-Way House, North End, and proprietor of the Elite Café, London Road, has been fined £5 with £10 guineas costs, for supplying false figures to the Ministry of Food and gaining more food points than he was entitled to.

William Harry Leppard of 47 Cantelupe Road, East Grinstead, said he was employed from February 1st to 6th by Mr. Greatorex, the East Grinstead Food Control Officer, to keep watch on the Elite Cafe and enter in a book the number of customers.

On February 1st there were 153, 2nd there were 161, 3rd there were 157, 4th there were 155, 5th there were 141 and on the 6th there were 126.

Miss Molly Fry of the East Grinstead Food Office estimated that the defendant was only entitled to 828 points, whereas on the number of meals he is purported to have served the Food Office issued him with 2,150 points.

The magistrate, Louisa Martindale, fined Bernard Richardson £5 with £10 guineas costs."

There were in all some 900 inspectors employed by the Ministry of Food. They quickly discovered that farmers and smallholders were the main source of producing food for the black market, but they seem to have made corner shop retailers their main target.

The national figures for successful prosecutions under the Food Control Order are remarkable. There were over 4,000 in the space of just two months during 1941.

Dying for a drink

Strong alcohol was in short supply during the war, and gangs made illegal 'hooch' using pure alcohol, industrial alcohol or methylated spirits mixed with flavours such as juniper and almond essences to make them palatable.

This stuff could prove lethal, and many victims were soldiers. The commanders of American camps in Britain issued their men with a free bottle of whisky or gin when they went on leave, just to keep them off the hooch.

Reluctant conscripts

Not everyone was keen to be 'called up' to serve his king and country. Indeed, many did everything they could to avoid it.

You had to be fit enough to serve in the forces, and one escape route was to persuade your doctor or your employer to issue you with a false certificate which said you had a disability of some sort.

Another scam was to pay someone else to turn up for the medical in your place – that someone, of course, being quite obviously in the very worst of health.

"Er, it says here that you're a lumberjack, Mr Smith..."

Food shops weren't the only outlets to be targeted. The general secretary of the National Association of Outfitters was soon complaining that small traders had become 'the most persecuted class in the whole of the country'.

Or was the *government* the most persecuted of them all? The fact is that it faced skulduggery at every turn and had to be on its guard all the time. Here are a few examples...

Bogus evacuees

At the outbreak of war it was decided that families in the countryside should be forced to take in evacuee children from the towns and cities. They would be given money to look after them – and this was, of course, another opportunity for the criminal fraternity.

Some hosts continued to claim their allowances long after the children had returned home. Even worse was the behaviour of people who stole blank billeting forms, invented names and drew allowances for completely fictitious evacuees.

Bombed out – 19 times!

The authorities came to the rescue of people who had been bombed out of their houses, giving them compensation to buy new things.

Unfortunately this was a great tempation to dishonest people, who realised that the national assistance office was overwhelmed with claims and therefore found it hard to check on all those queuing for help.

One man who WAS caught perpetrating what was known as 'the bomb lark' had claimed to have been made homeless 19 times in five months. He was jailed for three years.

Ghostly workers

One of the worst examples of large-scale fraud during the war involved a Liverpool ship repairer, Frederick Porter, who invented workers on his payroll so that he could claim money for their supposed work on non-existent jobs.

The scam made millions of pounds in today's values, the cash being stashed away in bank vaults all around the Lake District. When it was exposed a Liverpool councillor involved it in was sent to prison for nine years, a naval officer was sentenced to three years – and Frederick Porter shot himself.

An end at last?

There was such national rejoicing at the end of the war that the government actually made 'red, white and blue bunting available without use of coupons for one month'.

What generosity! And surely a dismantling of the tedious restrictions people had for so long endured must now follow?

Alas, no. There was a long, hard slog ahead.

"Don't they know there's not a war on?"

CHAPTER SIX

AFTER THE WAR WAS OVER

To everyone's relief the war ended in 1945, but the hardship was far from over. Bread and flour, which had never been restricted during the war, were put on the ration in July 1946.

There can have been no more depressing confirmation of something the British people had already come to realise – that military victory, however sweet it tasted at the time, had solved nothing economically.

The fallen

The immediate post-war world was a kind of wasteland, with an estimated 60 million people having been killed around the globe – two thirds of them civilians.

Arguing about the accuracy of the figures is not only pointless but distasteful. Some countries which registered smaller totals of deaths still lost far greater proportions of their populations (in Poland's case about 16 per cent).

Apart from these combined military and civilian deaths, many people died from famine and disease attributable to the war.

Soviet Union	27,000,000
China	12,000,000
Germany	8,000,000
Poland	6,000,000
Japan	2,500,000
Yugoslavia	1,700,000
Romania	1,000,000
France	800,000
Hungary	750,000
Austria	500,000
Greece	500,000
Italy	400,000
Czechoslovakia	400,000
United Kingdom	388,000
USA	300,000
Holland	250,000

The excitements, horrors and do-or-die sentiments of the war had gone, and in their place were only weariness, drabness and the same tedious, seemingly endless shortages. How could it be otherwise? All over the world, war-weary countries were attempting to rebuild their economies at a time of poor wheat harvests and serious shortages of butter, margarine and cooking fats.

The new bread rationing was complicated (it included cakes, buns and scones, too), but it meant that the ordinary 'man in the street' could expect just six slices a day. If that seems quite a bit more than you would expect to eat yourself, don't forget that there wasn't much else to take its place.

Bolshie Britain

How did people react? The Minister for Food, John Strachey, confidently told the House of Commons that 'if we read some of the accounts of the way the American public has been behaving in the last few weeks we should be glad that the government is going to even out distribution by rationing.

'We shall not have bodyguards round bakers' vans to prevent attacks from angry housewives. We shall manage things, we may hope, more decently and fairly.'

But something had changed in the public mood. The great war hero Winston Churchill had just lost the first post-war general election to Clement Attlee's Labour Party, partly because soldiers returning from the Front decided that those who had fought for their country should have more of a say in how it should be run. And the women, many of whom had done 'men's work' during the war, had a new-found confidence, too.

Revolting housewives

A Pathé newsreel about the introduction of bread rationing showed a Mrs Hilda Davis calling on 'an army of indignant housewives' to sign a petition against it, while 'a vicar's wife and food crusader', Mrs Lovelock, told a meeting of the British Housewives League that 'we, the housewives of Great Britain are in open revolt' and that 'the League will not stand for it'.

Mickey Mouse TV

Television closed down on 1st September 1939 after the broadcast of a Mickey Mouse film, 'Mickey's Gala Premiere'. When it started up again on 7th June 1946 the BBC chose to begin with the very same film – almost as if nothing had happened in the meantime!

There were only about 20,000 TV sets in those days, and you probably wouldn't have enjoyed a great many of the programmes, which were pretty 'worthy' overall.

Many echoed the much more popular radio programmes of the time, although the attempt to put on a version of 'How to Furnish a Flat' fell through, according to a BBC committee, 'owing to unavailability of the furniture'.

This post-war austerity extended to the best-loved children's programme of the period, 'Muffin the Mule'. He was a puppet – and you could see the strings moving!

Wot, no cartoons?

Nothing could be done about it, of course, and potato rationing (also unheard of during the war) was imposed during the following year. Things had actually got worse.

With the economy in a mess, unemployment rose from 400,000 to all of 1,750,000 in 1948. The government announced a freeze on wages ('If a lot of people want a larger slice they can only get it by taking it from others,' the chancellor the exchequer explained), and sport was banned during the week to prevent workers taking time off to watch it.

American aid

Help came (twice) from across the Atlantic. Between 1941 and 1945 the United States had given Britain war material worth a staggering $21 billion in a system known as lend-lease (we paid back the last instalment as recently as December 2006).

Now, between 1948 and 1951, the so-called Marshall Plan provided another huge sum to rejuvenate the economies of Europe. Soon we would turn the corner...

A royal wedding

The Roman satirist Juvenal said the only two things the public really wanted were 'bread and circuses'. Well, the British would have to wait until 1948 for unrationed bread, but they enjoyed the equivalent of a circus with the wedding of Princess Elizabeth (England's current queen) to Philip Mountbatten (now known as Prince Philip) in November, 1947. It was wonderful to have all this glorious razzmatazz in a time of austerity (including the famous golden coach), although there were a few 'humble' touches to show that the couple were in touch with reality:

- The government allowed the Princess 200 extra clothing coupons towards her trousseau (bridal outfit).
- The two royal prayer kneelers, covered in rose pink silk, were made from orange boxes and date-stamped 1916.
- Because of rationing, ingredients for the wedding cake were gifts sent from overseas.
- Other gifts from the public included a hand-knitted cardigan, two pairs of bed socks and a hand-knitted tea cosy.

Thank goodness for make do and mend!

One sad note was that Prince Philip's sisters weren't invited to the wedding. They were all married to Germans, and it was regarded as a bit too soon after the war for that. They did get to come, though, to the next grand occasion in London, the coronation of Queen Elizabeth in 1953.

Not to be sniffed at

Royal souvenirs were a novelty in 1947, and Buckingham Palace wasn't amused by some of the tat on sale to celebrate the royal wedding.

A plastic flag was said to amount 'almost to a caricature' (the manufacturers were advised to make the portraits on the flag more lifelike), while the uses to which a commemorative handkerchief might be put gave Palace staff the shudders.

The Home Office, however, ruled that the hankies were acceptable as buyers were unlikely to blow their noses on them.

An end to rationing

Most people who lived through those years regard the 1950s as a dismal, low-key decade lacking in colour, drive and self-confidence.

Things did improve, but very slowly (even in the early 1960s there were undeveloped bomb sites in London and other cities) and rationing went away only on 4th July, 1954 – by which time people had put up with nearly fifteen years of it.

Meat was the last foodstuff to be made freely available. Members of the London Housewives' Association held a special ceremony in Trafalgar Square, and Geoffrey Lloyd, the minister of fuel and power, burned a large replica of a ration book at an open meeting in his constituency.

Good riddance!

The festival of Britain

Austerity didn't disappear overnight, as we've seen, but the Festival of Britain, in the summer of 1951, was designed to mark a new era.

'The Festival is the British showing themselves to themselves – and the world,' said Herbert Morrison, the Labour MP who had been a major figure in its creation.

A new concert hall, the Royal Festival Hall, was built on the south bank of the Thames, while close to it were two structures which were designed to be only temporary – the Dome of Discovery and the slender, cigar-shaped Skylon.

The things Britain clearly wished to celebrate were its industry, science, landscape and character, although there was also a large funfair on the other side of the river in Battersea Park.

By the end of September more than eight million people had visited the Festival.

CHAPTER SEVEN

NEVER AGAIN?

Some of the lessons older people try to draw from their experience of the war years are bound to go in one of your headphoned ears and out of the other faster than a shard of shrapnel in an air raid:

- How can you leave that piece of potato skin/cabbage stalk/gristle on your plate when millions are starving?
- If you saved those bits of soap you've just thrown away you could make a new bar.
- In my day we'd make a pair of trousers last for years.
- You've left the bathroom light on yet again!
- Put a jumper on and you won't need to turn the central heating up.

173

In a time of plenty those penny-pinching ideas simply sound old-fashioned, and we're inclined to tell ourselves that we're too busy to give them much thought.

But wait a moment! Hard times may well be around the corner – and rationing is once again on the agenda.

Carbon footprints

In 2008 a House of Commons select committee proposed that every adult in Britin should be issued with an energy trading 'credit card'.

This would measure each individual's energy usage – or carbon footprint – whether at home or travelling. In short, how much you used would be capped (or rationed). You'd have to choose between, say, going on holiday or having the central heating on more often.

There would be a kind of market place, so that frugal people could be rewarded financially.

A report called 'A Rough Guide to Individual Carbon Trading' a couple of years earlier reached similar conclusions, and its authors said 'We could not find or imagine analogues in other fields of human activity for individual carbon trading beyond rationing during and after World War 2.'

The Environment Minister, Hilary Benn, turned the idea down because of its cost, but added that it was 'ahead of its time'. In other words: watch this space!

Martin's carbon footprint made him few friends.

The most attractive way of conserving precious energy is to offer incentives rather than to impose restrictions, and this is already happening in several areas. For example:

- Special lanes on busy roads for drivers carrying passengers rather than travelling alone.

- Supermarket rewards for customers who bring their own bags with them to avoid using plastic carriers.

- Grants for those who install wind turbines on their land or who insulate their lofts.

As for low-energy light bulbs, they're good for the planet, but as they flicker slowly into life nothing smacks more of wartime austerity!

Nor any drop to drink

These are useful initiatives, as are recycling schemes, 'eco cycles' on washing machines and the use of bio fuels, but something more drastic will be called for if the country runs short of water, as many of the experts fear.

What lessons would the government take from second world war rationing then?

First, the system it introduced would have to be regarded as fair – as was mainly so during the war.

Secondly it would have to be easy to manage, without the ability for the unscrupulous to exploit it, but as we've seen this is easier said than done.

Thirdly, the government would need to show more trust in the public than it was inclined to do before, with its intrusive snooping to catch out ordinary people breaking the law.

This may all be some way off, but one thing seems very likely: rationing may not follow the pattern experienced between 1940 and 1954, but in one form or another it will indeed eventually be with us again.

Woolton Pie, anyone?

GLOSSARY

Allied forces Men and women fighting on the side of the Allies, the group of countries opposed to Adolf Hitler's campaign of invasion. The Allies included the United Kingdom, the United States of America and the U.S.S.R along with many others.

Anderson shelter A small steel hut built to protect people from bomb blasts during the Blitz.

anthracite A dense, hard type of coal.

austerity A period in which a government is forced to drastically reduce its spending, leading to hard times for the people.

blackout A state in which lights had to be turned off or hidden behind thick blackout curtains in order to avoid drawing attention from enemy bombers overhead.

The Blitz The period of sustained bombing of Britain by the German Luftwaffe between 7th September, 1940 and 10th May, 1941.

census An official record of demographic information about a population.

dripping An animal fat produced from the fatty or otherwise unusable parts of cow or pig carcasses.

E-boat A fast German boat which fired torpedoes.

isinglass jelly A type of jelly made from fish.

Luftwaffe The German air force.

NAAFI The Navy, Army and Air Force Institutes, set up to provide entertainment for and to sell goods to servicemen.

surgical lint A type of fabric used in surgical dressings.

tallboy A piece of furniture incorporating a double chest of drawers and a wardrobe on top.

teasel head The spiky top of a teasel plant.

U-boat A German submarine used during World War I or World War II.

utility clothing/furniture Simplified and cheap products sold by the government at a fixed price during rationing.

wireless Equipment which could receive radio signals. Short for 'wireless telegraphy'.

WLA The Women's Land Army, a civilian organisation of women working in agriculture, replacing men called up to the military. Commonly called 'land girls'.

Rationing Timeline

1939

September 3rd War is declared.
September 22nd Petrol is rationed.
September 29th National register is set
    up and identity cards are issued.

1940

January 8th Butter, sugar, bacon and
    ham are rationed.
February 12th Paper is rationed.
March 11th Meat is rationed.
April 3rd Lord Woolton is appointed
    minister of food.
May 5th Strike action is banned.
May 8th Tea, margarine and cooking
    fats are rationed; ban on icing of
    confectionery; restaurants not
    allowed to serve fish and meat
    courses in the same meal.
May 10th Winston Churchill becomes
    prime minister.
May 27th Butter rations are cut.

June 18th–25th 'The graveyard week' for children's comics.

July 11th Public appeal for aluminium, collected by the WVS (Women's Voluntary Service.

July 20th Buying and selling new cars is banned.

July 23rd Emergency budget imposes higher taxes on luxury goods.

November 9th First looting convictions at the Old Bailey.

December 3rd Extra rations of tea and sugar for Christmas.

1941

March 17th Jam, marmalade, treacle and syrup are rationed.

April 8th United States enters the war.

April 19th Essential Work Order for women.

May 5th Cheese is rationed.

June 1st Clothing is rationed; egg distribution is controlled.

July 4th Coal is rationed.

November Milk distribution is controlled.

December National Dried Milk and
vitamin welfare scheme are
introduced; new points scheme for
food.

1942

January Rice and dried fruit are
rationed; tea ration for under-5s is
withdrawn.

February 9th Soap is rationed. Tinned
tomatoes and peas are rationed.

February 11th New law means black
marketeers face up to 14 years in
prison; National Loaf replaces white
bread.

February 17th Coal rationing is
extended to all domestic fuels.

June 1st Fripperies are banned on
clothing; American dried egg
powder goes on sale.

June 3rd Government takes over the
coal mines.

July 26th Sweets and chocolates are
rationed.

August Biscuits are rationed. Utility
furniture is introduced.

1943

March 7th Wings for Victory campaign launched.

July 29th Recruitment for women's services halted because more are needed for aircraft production.

September 24th Manpower crisis said to be looming.

October 29th Thames dockers on strike.

December 2nd Bevin Boys called up for the mines.

1944

February 1st Clothing restrictions lifted.

February 24th Miners are given a 4-year pay deal.

April 27th All foreign travel banned.

June 5 D-Day: Allied troops land in Normandy.

September 6th The blackout is relaxed.

September 17th 'Dim-out' replaces blackout.

October 8th New ministry of social insurance formed.

October 16th First British soldier demobilised.

November 20th Street lights turned on.

1945

April 24th 'Dim-out' abolished except in five coastal regions.

May 7th German High Command surrenders.

May 8th Victory in Europe Day.

June 13th New family allowances scheme announced.

July 5th General election held.

July 26th Election result declared: landslide victory for the Labour Party.

August 6th Atom bomb dropped on Hiroshima, Japan.

August 9th Atom bomb dropped on Nagasaki, Japan.

August 14th Japan surrenders.

August 17th Social reform programme announced by Labour, centred on NHS.

September 2nd Press censorship ends.

November 5th Dockers' strike ends.

1946

July 21st Bread and flour are rationed.

1947

November 8th Potatoes are rationed.
November 20th Wedding of Princess
      Elizabeth and Prince Philip.

1948

July 25th End of bread and flour
      rationing. End of potato rationing.
December End of jam rationing.

1949

March 15th End of clothes rationing.

1950

May 19th End of rationing for canned
      and dried fruit, chocolate biscuits,
      treacle, syrup, jellies and
      mincemeat.
May 26th End of petrol rationing.
September End of soap rationing.
October 3rd End of tea rationing.

1953

February End of sweets rationing.
March End of egg rationing.
April End of cream rationing.

June 2nd Coronation of Queen
Elizabeth 11.

September End of sugar rationing.

1954

May End of rationing of butter, cheese,
margarine and cooking fats.

July 4th End of all rationing as meat
becomes freely available in the
shops.

Index

More peculiar history from
The Cherished Library

Hankering for more triumphant tales of overcoming adversity? Look no further than *The Blitz: A Very Peculiar History*, by David Arscott, which tells a story of blackouts, Bletchley Park and bravery during the darkest (literally) period of World War II.

HB ISBN: 9781907184185

Author

David Arscott

David Arscott was a wartime
baby who survived the
London bombing, was briefly
evacuated to the north of
England and was later
brought up in a prefab
erected by German prisoners
of war. A former newspaper
journalist and BBC radio
producer, he has written
more than 40 books, both
fiction and non-fiction.